December 2007

Dear Laurie —

As you will no doubt recall, Sherri
McArdle, co-author of this book
was my executive coach for a
critical year during my career;
she taught me many valuable
lessons about how to become
my own personal best leader.
Over the course of that year, you
heard me pass along some of
her finest tips; better yet though,
here in this publication you can
now read them first-hand. I hope
you find this entertaining and
valuable!

Wishing you, always, wonderful
success along your leadership
journey,

KB

WHY DOGS WAG THEIR TAILS

WHY DOGS WAG THEIR TAILS

Lessons Leaders Can Learn About Work, Joy, and Life

Written by
Sherri McArdle and Jim Ramerman

an imprint of New Win Publishing
a division of Academic Learning Company, LLC

Copyright © 2007 by MRI Holding, LLC
Published by WBusiness Books,
an imprint of New Win Publishing,
a division of Academic Learning Company, LLC
9682 Telstar Ave. Suite 110, El Monte, CA 91731
www.WBusinessBooks.com

Cover Design by Gary Baltazar, Jr.

ISBN 10: 0-8329-5011-4
ISBN 13: 978-0-8329-5011-7

Printed in the United States of America
First Edition
11 10 09 08 07   1 2 3 4 5

Library of Congress Cataloging-in-Publication Data

McArdle, Sherri.
   Why dogs wag their tails: lessons leaders can learn about work, joy, and life/by
Sherri McArdle and Jim Ramerman.
      p. cm.
   ISBN 978-0-8329-5012-4
   1. Leadership.   2. Quality of work life.   3. Quality of life.   I. Ramerman, Jim.
II. Title.
HD57.7.M3952 2007
658.4'092—dc22

                    2007034860

CONTENTS

FOREWORD

Dogs are natural "connectors" – they tend to gravitate toward people, are open and responsive, and they usually let you know what they are feeling. There are no hidden agendas with the canine set.

No bones about it – it's pretty easy to know where a dog is coming from.

However, responding to them appropriately, giving them what they need, and helping them become the best dog they can be is another story. It's the same with people. And, it's the same with leadership.

That's where this book comes in.

Why Dogs Wag Their Tails: Lessons Leaders Can Learn About Work, Joy, and Life is an insightful book for leaders at all levels – from the CEO to the mid-level manager to anyone who has to assume a leadership role. It is a book written for those of us who truly want to create a great place to work.

I've worked with Sherri and Jim over the past ten years and they've helped me create a great place for people to work. In fact, my seventy-person marketing, advertising and public relations firm, located in upstate New York, has ranked on the Top 25 "Best Small Companies to Work for in America" list for three consecutive years. The list is produced by the Great Place to Work Institute and published in *HR Magazine,* the flagship publication of the Society for Human Resource Management (SHRM).

Sherri's and Jim's expertise, their earnest approach, and the accountability they foster in their clients have proven invaluable for my business. They've given me tools to help me focus on what's truly important for building a business, increasing morale, and generating a spirit of celebration and recognition in the workplace.

I remember meeting with Sherri for the first time. I was (I thought) quite prepared for this dialog and confidently explained to her how I approach each business day by waking very early and jotting down my to-do list. I proudly showed her that day's list with the typical one hundred or so items on it.

Sherri listened attentively, reviewed my list, and then asked a simple question: "How do you measure your success?" I responded enthusiastically by saying "By how many items I crossed off my list!"

You can probably guess where this conversation went.

Sherri encouraged me to rank the items on my list according to priority. Ultimately, the experience prompted me to hire an executive assistant to focus on many of the important things on my daily list, but not the essential ones that I needed to own as a leader to grow my business. This was an exercise in "Focus and Finish" – one explored more deeply in this book.

The book delves into other concepts that have also been important for me, including aligning my role as a leader with my top talents. By looking closely at my core competencies, I realized I needed to hire more people that complemented my skill set versus those who had personalities similar to mine.

Another concept is the importance of celebration, which is near to my heart and central to our agency culture. We do it at every level – from the huge, winding metal slide and "Primal Scream Room" in our office to summer sipper events with our clients to ski outings for the entire agency to having ice cream delivered to employees every Thursday in the summer to individual profit sharing.

Ultimately, this book affirms what Sherri and Jim have taught me – that leaders who can read people well, who make their cultures joyful, and who foster environments open to divergent ideas, are able to create an atmosphere in which others can truly benefit. The lessons in this book translate into real results: improved job performance, profits, and happier people.

So keep this book somewhere handy. If you're like me, you'll go back to it time and time again as a reminder of how to add more joy into your life and your work.

Lauren Dixon

Lauren Dixon
CEO
Dixon Schwabl Advertising, Inc.

High-Gain^{SM} Insights and Practical Ideas

When my business partner, Sherri McArdle, came to me with the idea for this book, there was no question in my mind that it was a terrific one. The nexus between dogs and the lessons of life is a natural one, so natural that I couldn't believe I hadn't thought of it myself – and this, of course, is the root of all great ideas. When you experience that "Why didn't I think of it first?" moment, you know that you've discovered something special. This book carries the force of epiphany, the power to transform the way people think, work, and live. As my daughter, Kristin, might put it: *This book is awesome!*

Two of the many important things I share with Sherri include the commitment and passion we have for our work as leadership consultants and the excitement we have for "applied sciences." On the one hand, we are grounded in the libraries and think tanks of great ideas; on the other hand, we are firmly grounded on the shop floors and in the offices and conference rooms of our clients. The deep enthusiasm we foster for our work comes from the real, honest, and powerful changes we've seen our clients invent in the laboratories of their own lives, both at work and at home.

For Sherri and me to be effective in our jobs, we need to be congruent — that is, to believe in and experience each and every recommendation we make to our clients. To quote Mahatma Gandhi, "We must become the change we seek in the world." That's the idea behind the High-Gain^{SM} Insights and Practical Ideas I've added after each of Sherri's chapters. You can use these sections as tools for achieving positive change for yourself — and for "becoming." These insights and ideas, joined with so many of Sherri's wonderful stories about people, dogs, and business, create an invaluable resource for those looking to find meaning in their lives and in their work. Like all great inventions, it's the idea and the practical application that bring it all together.

I love dreaming. I love creating. So why not dream *and* create? That's the challenge we all face today in an ever-more complex, ever-changing business environment. You can dream about what you want to become and what you want to achieve, and then you can take the positive steps necessary to build your vision. You have the power to create your own future. Sherri and I, through the stories and ideas we jointly put forth in this book, can help.

I am proud to have written the High-Gain^{SM} Insights and Practical Ideas segments of each chapter of *Why Dogs Wag Their Tails: Lessons Leaders Can Learn About Work, Joy, and Life.* These segments represent the culmination of many years of business consulting, a fervent immersion in the depths of diverse working environments, and countless lessons in the training room of life. To say that I support all the great wisdom in this book would be an understatement. I hope you enjoy the journey as much as I have.

– JIM RAMERMAN

ACKNOWLEDGEMENTS

Sherri McArdle

I would like to thank my beloved Bichon Frise, Scout, for teaching me, day in and day out, what leadership means (even if it is the hard way sometimes) and for his constant inspiration and unconditional love. I would like to thank Bob Minchella, my dog trainer, for showing me how to become the leader Scout needed me to be and especially for his direct feedback and sense of humor when I needed it. I would like to thank George Gazarek for planting the seed for writing this book on New Year's Eve when he first heard me talk about it. I would also like to thank Elaine St. James for firing me up to write this book with her enthusiasm for this project on a long walk in Santa Barbara.

I would like to thank all of our clients, colleagues, family, and friends who inspired me in their remarkable ways, and by their work, stories, and enthusiasm for this project. A very special thank you to those people whose personal stories we used with their permission: Terry McArdle, Ron Spingarn, Father Jim Callan, Jim Smith, and Paul Hudson. I would like to thank all of the generous dog owners and their wonderful dogs for showing me how canines can teach us about ourselves, and how to become better at life and at work if we are willing to listen. Special thanks to BJ Mann and her well-trained dogs, Kayla, Cody, and Spirit; Jenna Rawlins and her dog Diamond; Sharon Gordon and her dogs Bailey and Maggie; Vicki and Myron Liebhaber and their magnificent dog Logan; Steve Schwartz and Alice Tariot and their dog Milo; Adam and Carrie Grossman and their dog Jack; Jamie Schuster and his dogs Roxie and Sydney; Erin Martin and her dog Libby; and Karen and Ken Baker and their energetic dog Blaze.

I would like to thank Nick DiChario for his talented editing, encouraging style, and his "can do" attitude, a rare combination. Thank you to our agent Ken Lizotte, our attorney Mark Costello and to the team at WBusiness Books. Thank you to my business partner, Jim Ramerman, and the McArdle Ramerman team—Terry, Peg, Erin, Alissa, Judy and Francine—for their talents, contributions and support in the wonderful work they do for our clients every day. A special thank you goes to Peg Mercier for her ongoing dedication to our firm and for her amazing attention to all of the details of this project.

My deepest thanks are to my husband Terry, and our children Matt and Rachel, for their incredible support, love, and encouragement, and for listening to yet another dog story. They are truly remarkable (and patient) people.

Jim Ramerman

My thanks to the wonderful canines in my life who brought me great love: Cisco, my first dog, a Dalmatian, was named after *The Cisco Kid*—a 1950s TV Western. Once when I was lost in the woods at six-years old, my dad found me only because he could see Cisco's black-and-white spots leaping well above my head. Hogan, the puppy my family adopted while I was in junior high, was half Basset, quarter Beagle, and quarter Cocker. He was named after Colonel

Hogan in the 1960s TV comedy *Hogan's Heroes*. This wonderful mutt was eccentrically popular as the underdogs of the world can sometimes be.

Most especially, I thank Terra, my family's purebred Golden Retriever, who has taught me the most about myself and about life because of who she is and maybe because this student was finally ready.

Along with Sherri, I thank the tremendous team at McArdle Ramerman, Inc., who make so much possible—you are each so incredibly talented in what you do and are the wind beneath our wings. I join Sherri in appreciation of Nick DiChario. He is a rare individual, a talented writer and editor, and a joy to work with beginning to end.

Thanks to my family, friends, and clients who have given me all the reason in the world to celebrate life. Because of them I've wagged my tail often, long, and vigorously.

For the record, Sherri is the driving force and main author of this work. My thanks for her partnership, her boundless energy, and her passion to deliver results. She has helped a lot of us—clients, family, and friends—answer a lot of life's important "why" questions.

People, Dogs, Life, Work

Ralph Nader once said, "I enjoy my work so much that I have to be pulled away from my work into leisure." Do the people you know talk about their jobs with that kind of passion? Do your friends and family love their work so much that they have to be pulled away from it? Do you?

Some people are working much harder than they would like to work and want more time to spend with their families. Some people are stressed by the pressures and the pace of change. Some feel unprepared to perform at new levels, while others are in the wrong positions and would do something else if they only had the opportunity. Some are coping by disconnecting emotionally from work and from their loved ones.

Clearly, there must be a better way.

Why Dogs?

From the East Coast (where I live) to the West Coast (where I often visit) to Europe (where I wish I could visit more), I can tell you that many people I've met love their dogs. They walk them with pride. They take them to work, if and when they can. They bring them to restaurants, shopping areas, and outdoor cafés. They introduce them to people as if they're members of the family. More and more, dogs have become part of our everyday lives and landscapes. Today, Americans as a whole own nearly seventy-four million dogs.

Dogs are great companions and great teachers. They teach us about ourselves: our humanity, our compassion, and our tolerance. I've learned firsthand that dogs can also teach us how to be happier in our lives and our careers.

Several years ago, I surprised myself. My family and I got a dog, Scout, and I started watching him closely. I began gaining insights into many things canine and human.

One of the first things Scout taught me about was the power of smiling. I smile when I think of Scout. When I smile, my mental state changes. I become more relaxed and more approachable. When I'm in a more relaxed and approachable state, I connect better with people, and I'm more encouraging. My dog Scout has taught me a lot about being a more effective and happier person at home and at work. He was my inspiration for this book.

I've noticed that my clients relax when they talk about their dogs. Their eyes light up, their body language softens, and they are at peace, suddenly and profoundly, without even thinking about it. The powerful connection they have with their dogs outweighs their problems and stress on the job. They connect with me on a more intimate basis. We talk about the adventures we've had with our dogs and how much we've learned from them and about ourselves.

For dogs, there is no such thing as work, and they don't need a handbook for living. Instead, they rely on their instincts, the structure placed around them, and the leadership that directs them, either from people or a pack leader.

For people, there's life and work. Nobody gives us a handbook for how to live or work effectively. We rely on our intuition, our experience, and the structure and leadership we have been given.

Dogs need to be led by good leaders. They require structure in which to operate effectively. They want to be good followers. When they don't sense leadership, they fill the void and try to assume it.

People need good leadership and structure in order to operate effectively. They want to work for good leaders and follow good leaders. When people don't sense strong leadership, they, too, try to fill the void, either consciously or unconsciously.

My business partner Jim Ramerman and I both have beloved dogs. Scout is my family's wonderful and energetic Bichon Frise. Jim's family has Terra, a sleek, intelligent, and loving Golden Retriever. In fact, everyone on our team at work has had dogs in their lives at one time or another. Dogs are special creatures. They are the perfect companions. Loyal. Playful. Intent. Loving. Fully engaged in the moment. They reflect back to us so much about ourselves. If we watch them, if we listen to them, dogs can help us become better people at work and at home. Dogs can teach <u>us</u> new tricks.

I decided to use the lessons I've learned in developing leaders over many years, and the lessons Scout has taught me in my daily life, to make some very interesting connections among people, dogs, life, and work. Some of the principles you'll read about I have been working on with clients for years, and I've discovered that dogs pick up on them naturally. Other behaviors I discovered through Scout (and other dogs) and simply began applying them to work situations. The people with whom I've worked have applied these principles with great success in their careers, and I believe that you can apply them in yours, too.

Napoleon Bonaparte once said, "A dog teaches us a lesson in humanity." Who doesn't need that from time to time?

*   *   *

I've run an executive- and leadership-development firm with my business partner – Jim Ramerman – for the past twelve years. We've worked with CEOs, senior executives, and people throughout the workforce, logging more than twenty-thousand hours of High-Gain conversations with individuals in every corner of the marketplace, including public, private, not-for-profit, and family-owned businesses, as well as multinational corporations. After many hours of conversations, I've discovered that far too many people are unhappy with different aspects of their lives and work.

Dogs, on the other hand, are happy naturally. Dogs overcome their adversities, no matter what life deals them. Dogs are remarkable for their joy and playfulness, their capacity to keep learning, and their resilience.

Every so often, we come across some very remarkable people, too. Some have found joy in learning new job skills they never thought they could master. Others have found great satisfaction in increasing their sense of self-worth and learning how to cope with change. Still others have taken risks they never thought themselves capable of until they looked at themselves in new and interesting ways.

Throughout this book, you'll read humorous and heartwarming stories about interesting people and remarkable canine companions. You'll meet the incredibly joyful spinning dog, Ruby, and Logan, the regal Collie Club champion. In Chapter 5, you'll discover how Terry brought joy back to his work when he discovered he could choose his boss. In Chapter 11, you'll meet a brilliant young man named Kenny, who is overcoming a learning disability to achieve remarkable personal goals. You'll get a glimpse into the lives of dogs and people and, along the way, you'll gain valuable insights into work and life.

All the stories here are true, or based on actual events. Sometimes they are a compilation of more than one situation. I have changed names, genders, companies, and details whenever necessary to uphold our pledge of confidentiality to clients and colleagues, a vital tenet of our work.

I hope you will read with interest, answer the High-Gain questions at the end of each chapter, and actually take the steps to implement the valuable lessons you learn. This book will help you do all of that, if you're willing.

One final thought: It's not essential for you to have a dog of your own to get something out of this book. You don't necessarily have to be a "dog person," for that matter, although chances are if you've read this far into the introduction, you've known at least one dog closely in your life.

What it comes down to, I believe, is this:

If you have the capacity in your heart to love, to be passionate about something dear to you, these stories will reveal their secrets. Rest assured that you already have the inherent ability to make positive changes in your life and work. You will come to see that there are many reasons dogs wag their tails and, that by learning a little about these marvelous animals, you may learn quite a bit about yourself. In fact, you may even learn how to wag your tail, too.

CHAPTER 1

Keep On Learning

I was the last holdout in my family when it came to the decision about getting a dog. My husband, Terry, had known two wonderful dogs, Pinky and Schooner, both mutts. Pinky had been the dog of his early childhood and, as such, had been a special part of the family. His mother got Schooner when Terry was older, and I grew to love Schooner after I met Terry.

Our two children fantasized about getting a dog, as most children do. They made all the usual noises about how the dog would be *their* responsibility, how *they* would walk it and feed it and clean up after it, and do whatever needed to be done so Mom and Dad wouldn't get stuck with all the chores.

I knew right from the start, of course, that this was bunk. I'm a practical person. Working at a marriage, raising two children, and running a leadership-consulting business was plenty for me to manage, and I didn't want to take on a pet, too. So I hemmed, hawed, and delayed the inevitable for as long as possible, until I finally warmed up to the idea (or cracked under the pressure), although to this day I'm not even sure I could tell you why.

The next consideration was our oldest daughter, Rachel, who was allergic to dogs and cats. Terry took on the research of finding hypoallergenic breeds, and we settled on the Bichon Frise. We found a reputable breeder in upstate New York, and soon after, became the parents of an energetic, white puffball of a male Bichon pup. Our son, Matt, named him Scout.

Scout was born in the year 2000 on Labor Day weekend, with a built-in connection to work (the labor part) that had escaped me at the time. I believe Bichons have a high "adorability factor"; that is, they are made so people will fall in love with them, and then all rules go out the window. Adding Scout to the family was like adding another child to the household. And as with human babies, the early months weren't exactly easy.

I remember standing outside on many cold nights, snowflakes falling in the moonlight, while I waited for Scout to pee for the tenth time in two hours. (Telling a dog to hurry up about it, by the way, is a complete waste of time.) After eight months of this, Scout was finally housebroken, or so we thought.

We installed a doggie door on the patio so he could go in and out at will. He had the run of the house during the day while we were at work. He often napped on our beds so he could look out the window from the second floor and watch the world go by. He sat on our laps in the family room, satisfying all those baby cravings for me, and providing lots of affection for our children.

For the next five years, my life was full of the usual challenges of raising two kids and running a company. Everyone in the family was busy. Rachel went off to college. Matt played sports and attended middle school. Terry left his job at a large corporation and eventually joined my firm. My business grew into a well-respected leadership- and executive-development corporation in upstate New York.

This, however, was not the end of the story.

We've Got a Problem

 The supposedly housebroken Scout began peeing all over the house. I know that may not be a pleasant thought, but if you've ever lived with a dog in your life, you understand that many things come with pet ownership, including cleaning up the occasional accident.

I would find the places he "went" almost weekly. I suppose I was aware of what was happening, yet the magnitude of the issue seemed to creep up on me in slow motion. This is often the case with recognizing issues at work too, as you will discover later on in this book.

The vet assured us that there was no medical problem. Scout did not have a urinary-tract infection, which I sort of hoped would be the answer, as that would have meant we could solve it with medication. But our Western philosophy of "let's fix it now with meds" didn't extend to the animal kingdom this time.

We had just redecorated the house with nice furniture, which he was now ruining unashamedly, and I was growing increasingly frustrated. We could never catch Scout in the act, and no amount of after-the-fact scolding worked either.

One day I was lamenting about the problem with a friend, and she suggested I see a dog behaviorist in town, a highly respected expert named Bob. I eagerly (OK, frantically!) placed the call, and after trading several messages, we finally connected. He was clearly busy and in demand. To the best of my recollection, here is how our conversation went:

Bob: So what's the problem you're having with Scout?

Sherri: Scout is a five-year-old Bichon. Over the last six months he's been urinating all over the house: in the dining room, in the family room, and even on our bed. I've had him checked out by the vet, and he's fine, no urinary-tract problems.

Bob: OK. Have there been any other big things going on at home?

Sherri: No.

Bob: Have there been other changes in his behavior?

Sherri: No.

Bob: I think I know what the problem is. You're having a leadership issue.

Sherri: (Laughing) Do you know what I do for a living?

Bob: No.

Sherri: I own a leadership firm.

Bob: (Laughing) Physician, heal thyself.

Sherri: How soon can we get together?

Bob: The sooner, the better. For your sake.

The first session with Bob was an eye-opener. When he entered the house, he never looked at Scout or acknowledged him. He didn't pet him or touch him. Consequently, Scout did not do his usual jump-and-bark routine.

Terry, Matt, and I sat on the couch across from Bob, and Scout jumped onto the couch with us, lying down. Bob sat across from us and commented on how calm a Bichon Scout seemed to be. He asked if Scout was always this way.

"No," I replied. In fact, I had never seen Scout so relaxed around a stranger.

After spending a little time observing Scout and getting to know him, Bob said that Scout had taken the dominant position in the house, and we needed to reclaim our authority. He said that we were not going to like what he was about to suggest. He also said that some people didn't follow his advice because it meant making changes with their dog that they didn't want to make.

I grimaced, waiting for the other shoe to drop. I wasn't sure what Bob was going to say next. I braced myself for the worst.

Bob assured me that Scout's problem could be solved if we were willing to make some changes. Those changes included the following:

1. Scout would no longer be able to sleep on our bed.

2. Scout should not sit on our laps anymore.

3. Scout should not run up the stairs ahead of us.

4. Scout would need training in some simple "sit," "stay," and "down" commands.

My husband Terry is the natural alpha male in our family pack, and Scout obeyed him unquestioningly from the start. Knowing how to handle a dog comes easily to Terry. It seems I was more of "a problem." Scout didn't see me as an authority figure. Looking back, I would have flunked doggie training. I referred to Scout as "my last baby" and treated him accordingly. I never established good dog boundaries. Scout became a full member of our household with all the privileges of membership.

In her wonderful book *The Natural History of Love*, Diane Ackerman writes, "Once a pet enters a household, it enters the family dynamics, and that can be either good or bad, depending on the people involved." For me, it turned out to be both good and bad.

Unintentionally, I had reinforced Scout's dominant behaviors and sent the wrong messages about what I would tolerate (another leadership issue). Scout, for his part, was just being himself and taking my apparent cues that he was in charge. Like the wolf descendent he was, he had simply marked his territory and worked his way up our household chain of command.

As heartbreaking as it was to think about no longer having a lap dog, I decided that it would be worse if he were to continue ruining the furniture.

Under Bob's tutelage, I started training Scout, and I begrudgingly made all the changes he suggested. Scout stopped urinating all over the house. As I stepped up my leadership with Scout, it was as if I had turned off his faucet.

Bob and I started meeting with Scout for regular training sessions. I'm the boss now and Scout is respecting my authority. Training isn't easy for either of us. I don't always get the commands right or the timing down, but I continue to work at it "doggedly."

I'm becoming the leader that Scout needs me to be.

And yes, you can teach old dogs new tricks. Take it from me.

An Old Dog Learns New Tricks

 Dogs (old or young) aren't the only ones capable of learning new tricks. Anyone in business can and should develop this survival skill. Just ask Frank.

Frank was a nationally respected executive with a thirty-year career in his field. He gave talks and published papers. People listened when Frank spoke. He had a soft but authoritative voice and a distinguished manner about him. He was also incredibly knowledgeable, focused, and disciplined. Ironically, he was more respected outside his company than inside when we started working together.

Frank's responsibilities were changing. His business unit was consolidated with several others under one large umbrella. It was becoming more important for him to add new clients and develop his people to support a growing business. While his technical skills were highly respected, his credibility within the company was now being tested because the business results weren't up to par. Frank knew it. His boss Alan knew it. Alan's peers knew it. And the CEO knew it.

Alan had always believed in Frank. They'd worked together for almost twenty years and were very similar in nature. Like Frank, Alan thought everyone was a professional. Alan and Frank assumed people knew what needed to be done and would figure out how to do it. Neither of them had developed their people much nor liked conflict, so performance issues went unaddressed for long periods.

Both took their time in deliberating the issues of the day, often with each other. As a result, in the eyes of the increasingly business-focused executives, they were seen as slow decision-makers. Alan and Frank came across as cautious and tentative during intense business discussions about how to raise revenue and attack markets. Pressure was growing on both of them; their ability to change wasn't keeping pace with the crisis.

I met Frank and got to know him and the issues facing him. I suggested that he start getting feedback about his effectiveness from people in the company. As a result of our conversations, he began to develop some deeper insights into himself and his role in both the problems facing the company and in the solutions he would have to find.

It wasn't easy for Frank to ask for feedback and to acknowledge his shortcomings. A proud and religious man, Frank had built his career on his credibility and a strong set of personal values. Now his credibility was being questioned. We met several times to talk through the issues.

One day Frank declared, "I have to move beyond consensus leadership and elevate this business problem to a crisis level in the minds of the people who work for me. It's up to me to see that they make more rapid corrections."

As he said this, Frank sat upright in his chair. He stared straight ahead with his hands folded in his lap, unblinking. He was a neatly groomed man, wearing beige pants and a blue blazer. His presence was often gentle and quiet, so when he made his declaration it caught me by surprise – and I was glad to hear it.

"I've been reactive to problems," he said, "not anticipating them. I've been tentative about making changes. Consequently, I haven't been able to influence the organization cross-functionally. People respect me technically, but they don't respect me as a businessman."

"You haven't been getting the level of business results the company needs," I suggested. "You're getting lost in project details. You're going to have to do some unlearning and new learning if you want to rise to the challenge. You'll need to let go of some of those projects you love and learn to become passionate about the business of acquiring and leading projects through others."

"You know," he said, "this has become a fundamentally different job from the one I accepted. I've been growing increasingly tentative, which breeds tentativeness in others, and then their support for my leadership wanes."

"What would help increase your effectiveness?" I asked.

Silence . . . a thoughtful hesitation. "I want to become clear about what I need to do to build this business. I want to figure out how to break into a huge new industry and to become an integrated solution provider."

"Where should you start?"

"Well, I'm pretty familiar with the industry. The problem is that I haven't figured out how to apply what I know about the industry creatively or innovatively."

"Who can help you figure that out?" I asked.

"I know three guys who are nationally recognized industry experts outside of the company. I could start with them."

"Would they do some brainstorming with you?"

"I could ask," Frank said a bit tentatively.

"Why are you hesitating?" I asked.

"I've never had to reach out to them in this way," Frank said quietly. "I usually see them at conferences where I'm speaking or they're speaking, and it's just a whole different environment. I guess I feel funny about asking them for help."

"Is that how you see it? A desperate plea for them to save you?"

That got a smile out of him. Sometimes when I hit the fear with a hammer, I can bang it into an insight.

"My guess is," I went on, "if you raise your clarity about what you need, if you're confident in your ability to attack it, and if you have strong convictions about the importance of building this business, any one of them would be happy to talk to you. You'd be opening up, Frank, being inclusive. If you really think about it, you'd be aligning with your personal values, not contradicting them."

Frank took in the suggestion and nodded in agreement. I imagined he was processing the input and already figuring out how he could make those phone calls.

Frank focused on developing his most mission-critical skills over the next few years. These included driving himself and his team to higher levels of results, confronting underperformers in positive and encouraging ways, recruiting talent to fill specific needs within the organization, and developing his staff.

The business didn't turn around right away. Alan continued to get a lot of pressure about Frank. But Alan's support for Frank was unwavering. He never caved in when his peers suggested Frank be repositioned or terminated. His instincts told him to wait it out.

Meanwhile, Frank persevered. He was not a quitter, and he always had a strong faith in himself and his abilities. Frank's prospecting efforts started to bear fruit within a year. He landed two of the largest pieces of business the company had ever had. He stirred a few pots by letting his people know where they needed to improve. One by one, he also added new levels of talent to his team.

Alan's patience paid off. He continued to encourage Frank and gave him the room he needed to grow. Frank's dedication to the company and his willingness to learn and apply new skills was a powerful combination. Frank is now one of the company's stars.

Frank recently told me that he felt like a kid again. "Isn't it great," he said, "that at this stage in my career I can still learn and grow and make a difference?"

Just as Scout and I had found new tricks to change old habits, Frank, too, had learned that he could adjust to his changing business environment. Frank still reminds himself that his development needs to continue, that even highly educated and credible people benefit from help once in a while. And Alan, for his part, continues to remind his peers not to be in such a hurry to give up on "old dogs."

High-Gain Insights

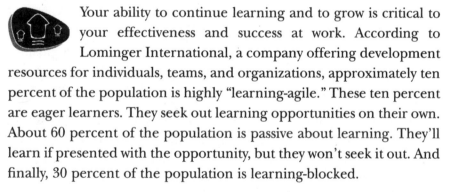 Your ability to continue learning and to grow is critical to your effectiveness and success at work. According to Lominger International, a company offering development resources for individuals, teams, and organizations, approximately ten percent of the population is highly "learning-agile." These ten percent are eager learners. They seek out learning opportunities on their own. About 60 percent of the population is passive about learning. They'll learn if presented with the opportunity, but they won't seek it out. And finally, 30 percent of the population is learning-blocked.

If you work on increasing your learning agility in many directions – people agility, mental agility, results agility, and change agility – your organization will regard you as having higher potential and is more likely to offer you opportunities for advancement.

For those committed to becoming learning-agile, here are some questions to ask yourself:

1. How eager are you to learn and grow?

2. How learning-agile are you, and in what ways?

3. How can you increase your learning agility and what would the benefits to you and your organization be?

4. What skills or special knowledge would you like to pursue that you don't currently possess?

5. What skills that you already possess would you like to update or strengthen?

6. In what ways can you more actively seek development?

Once you've answered these questions, you can begin to form a learning plan, either on your own or with the help of your supervisor, manager, or human resources and training departments. You'll be amazed by the positive reaction you will receive at work when you show an eagerness to learn and grow.

Practical Ideas

- Be interested in people, especially new and diverse people (e.g., people in different professional fields) and act on that interest. Start conversations with them and ask many respectful, yet probing questions.

- Read books and articles on the latest breakthroughs in your field. Even more important, read magazines from other, unrelated fields. This will keep your brain growing and agile, and will open your mind to creative insights.

"Learning is not attained by chance. It must be sought for with ardor and attended to with diligence."

– ABIGAIL ADAMS

CHAPTER 2

Earning Credibility

Scout's track record in the pee department is pretty straight-forward. Either he has stopped urinating in the house, or he hasn't. The same holds true for his other issues. Either he follows my commands when we're walking, or he doesn't. Either he waits for me at the bottom of the stairs, or he doesn't. Scout's credibility with me must be earned every day on a case-by-case basis.

You may look at your job in the same way. Every day at work, your credibility will be challenged. You will be asked to perform your daily duties, the tasks you've been trained to do, to a high level of expertise without constant supervision. If you perform well, you will, in all likelihood, be rewarded with more tasks and higher expectations. This is the way most of us earn credibility and move ahead at work.

Your credibility is an important part of your effectiveness and ultimate success or failure at work. Credible people perform at higher levels and drive higher performance in others. People want to work with and for credible people. Credibility is in the eye of the beholder. It's not about what you think of yourself; it's about what others think about you. Credibility can and should be earned through hard work, dedication, and honesty. Much like trust, if it's broken, credibility is hard (although not impossible) to restore.

Actions Bark Louder Than Dogs

 For Brad, his credibility issues became his undoing.

Brad was recruited into the manufacturing division of a large privately held company. His résumé was impeccable. Ivy League schools. Public-company experience. Operations-and-sales background. He had lived in various parts of the country and the world. Brad was being courted by several companies, and he chose this job because he'd had enough of traveling and wanted to settle down in a nice community with his wife and four children. He hoped he could show Tim, his new boss, what he could do, and he had aspirations of becoming a partial owner of the business. They'd talked about this and many other goals during the interview.

Tim, the CEO, proudly introduced Brad to the manufacturing team on Brad's first day. Brad was assertive and outgoing, a man who seemed to have little trouble fitting in socially or professionally. He had a firm handshake and a big smile.

Everything started out well enough. Tim had told Brad, "Look, we'll get together whenever you want so I can show you the ropes and teach you the business. But for the most part, I'm going to leave you alone when it comes to your team. Do things your way. That's why I hired you, after all. If you want my advice, let me know."

That was twelve months ago, before things started to unravel. When Tim began hearing that his people in operations weren't happy with their new boss, he dismissed this as rumor. But he couldn't dismiss the people from the manufacturing team who were coming directly to him.

"The guy thinks he's so smart, he just tells us what to do."

"The guy thinks he's so smart, he just tells us what to do."

"He doesn't ask our opinions or listen to what we have to say. We've been around a lot longer than he has, and maybe we know a few things, too."

"He's making changes all over the place, but where's his plan?"

"We're moving too fast! It's chaotic down on the floor. Doesn't he see the product-quality problems coming?"

"We've nicknamed him 'The Hurricane.' He comes through, messes things up, and goes back to his office, leaving a wake of problems behind him."

Brad was a guy with a lot of ideas. He saw many things that needed doing and wanted to start making changes. Because he was a quick learner, he spotted problems and usually had plenty of ideas about how to fix them.

Tim was more the quiet, confident type. He dressed conservatively, spoke not to impress people, but only when he needed to communicate something, and could often be found at the outskirts of a conversation rather than at its center. He was the kind of person who thought things through, and when he made a decision, he usually stuck with it. He was highly optimistic but a bit concerned when he asked me to work with Brad. He'd never seen the guys in manufacturing riled up like this before. He tried to talk with Brad, but Tim didn't like confrontation, so he was pretty indirect about it.

Brad wasn't really getting the message, and Tim wasn't really delivering it to him.

Brad was eager to work with me. He considered it a perk and a sign that Tim had confidence in him.

Tim had told Brad that he had complete confidence in his abilities and was sure that whatever issues had come up with the manufacturing team, they could be resolved.

The leadership assessment, however, revealed some significant issues that had been developing over Brad's acrimonious tenure:

1. When Brad began, he didn't ask many questions or take the time to learn the manufacturing operation from the people who knew it best.

2. Brad often tried to come off as if he knew things he didn't know. The team saw through this and lost respect for him.

3. Brad was not an inclusive leader, something the manufacturing team had grown accustomed to with Brad's predecessor. He made decisions pretty much on his own and then informed the team.

4. The team was worried that Brad wasn't telling Tim what the reports didn't yet show: while they were meeting their production goals, product quality was starting to dip. They knew that they were unlikely to see the gains in production they had projected for the second half of the year because too many changes were going to slow things down.

5. Brad liked nice things. He decorated his office in a way that seemed a bit out of character on the floor, even though he said he did it on a shoestring. He also liked nice cars, and when Tim let him lease one, the model he chose stood out from the others in the parking lot.

Brad tried to minimize the importance of the report when he first saw it. He kept a confident air, joked around a bit, and looked too relaxed in his chair. He was sure that people were over-scrutinizing him, people who didn't know what to make of him because he was new and trying to do new things.

"It's more complicated than people being upset about the changes you're making," I suggested to Brad. "I'm hearing that people are unhappy with how you're making those changes and the way you're interacting. Were you aware of how your people were feeling?"

"I've worked in a lot of places, and it's not abnormal for people to be upset when they have to change. I've heard some grumbling, but that's to be expected. It's not unusual for people to get mad at the guy making the changes."

I was growing increasingly concerned with Brad's nonchalant attitude. I was starting to think this was more serious than Brad was acknowledging. If this was the way he reacted to confidential and pointed feedback, what was he like when his team disagreed with him directly?

"Brad," I said uneasily, "I'm not sure you're getting the implications of this for your leadership. I think you may have a credibility problem with your team. It could be serious. It might be repairable, but only if you accept it and work hard at restoring it."

I suggested we get together with Tim to talk some more. Brad agreed, and the following week the three of us met. Brad shared the full report with Tim in advance of the meeting.

Tim didn't like what he had read. He put on an optimistic and positive face with Brad, but I could see he was worried. I knew him well enough to know he wasn't happy. I'm sure he was wondering if he'd made the right decision bringing Brad onboard, whether he'd let him have too much autonomy too soon, and whether he'd be to blame because he hadn't acted quickly enough to stop the bleeding.

Brad said pretty much the same things to Tim as he'd said to me at our previous meeting. Brad still didn't see that he had a credibility problem, and he wasn't sure there was anything much he needed to do differently except trade in his car for something more acceptable. Brad had plenty of strengths. He was brash and confident and had flair. He was daring and willing to take chances. He was never short of creative solutions. These were all good leadership qualities.

But Brad had a serious downside. He often ran too hard and fast, like a horse with blinders on, not really watching where he was going or caring about the other horses on the track. These qualities showed lack of leadership, disregard for consequences, and a tendency toward immature impulses.

Tim asked Brad if he wanted to continue working with me.

"Yes," Brad said, and I could detect the slightest bit of frustration in his tone. My guess was that he was doing this for Tim, and he was getting tired of it. He couldn't see any real value in it anymore. This was a very bad sign.

A couple of weeks later, when I asked my secretary if Brad had called to make another appointment like he said he would, nobody had heard from him. Our administrator had tried to call him, but he hadn't returned the call.

Tim and I continued to meet for our regular appointments. I always asked how things were going with Brad. "Up and down," he would say.

Six months later, Tim told me he let Brad go. I wasn't at all surprised. I asked him if it was difficult decision for him to make.

He shook his head sadly and said, "I knew things didn't look good the day I read that report. But I wanted him to be successful. I wanted to give the guy the benefit of the doubt. I liked Brad, I really did. I just couldn't let it go on any longer. His stubbornness was bringing down a company that took me years to build. I really didn't have a choice."

"How did your team react to the firing?" I asked.

"I knew I'd done the right thing when the manufacturing team came up and thanked me for making the tough call. They said the guy never had established credibility with them, and they were eager to help in any way they could until I found a replacement for him. I only wish I'd done it six months earlier."

"You might not have felt as good about it six months earlier," I told him.

"True. It's not that I feel that great about it now. After all, I'm the guy who has to take responsibility for making a mistake and hiring the wrong man for the job. As a result of that, we're going to be digging ourselves out of a pretty deep hole for a while."

"Yes, but look at the upside. You've earned a lot of respect and credibility from your people by doing the right thing. In the end, it may just bring you all closer together."

Tim agreed.

High-Gain Insights

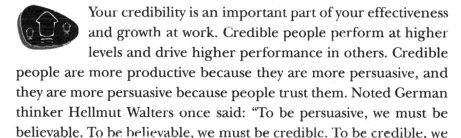 Your credibility is an important part of your effectiveness and growth at work. Credible people perform at higher levels and drive higher performance in others. Credible people are more productive because they are more persuasive, and they are more persuasive because people trust them. Noted German thinker Hellmut Walters once said: "To be persuasive, we must be believable. To be believable, we must be credible. To be credible, we must be truthful."

Credibility is never overlooked in the business world. Even if people can't always define this quality in others, they will always recognize and respond to it either consciously or subconsciously. In short, credibility equals success.

Here are a few principles that we use in guiding our clients when it comes to credibility:

1. People want to work with and for credible people.

2. Credibility is in the eye of the beholder. It's not about what you think of yourself, it's about what others think about you.

3. Credibility can be earned. But if it's broken, it's hard (but not impossible) to restore.

There are three ways to increase your credibility at work. Consider how you would measure yourself on each of the following credibility principles:

1. Do you live by a set of unquestionable moral and ethical values under all working conditions – every time?

2. Do you take on roles that suit your talents and passion, and then eagerly take your skills to the highest level?

3. Do you create, with unfaltering consistency, a personal history of meaningful outcomes and results?

Practical Ideas

- Before you commit to an assignment, make sure that your capabilities match the challenge.

- Be certain that you are committed to the assignment.

- Write down what you will do and when you will have it completed.

- Remember to under-promise and over-deliver. Whatever people expect of you, go one better, e.g., before the due date, better quality, do it with more enthusiasm, etc.

"Whatever the job you are asked to do at whatever level, do a good job because your reputation is your résumé."
– Madeleine Albright

"Don't accept your dog's admiration as conclusive evidence that you are wonderful."
– Ann Landers

CHAPTER 3

Have a Plan to Achieve Your Goals

John is a great craftsman. He's the kind of guy so comfortable with tools you'd swear he was born with them in his hands. When he's working, he really focuses on the job. Sometimes, he enjoys a good conversation, especially when you put a cup of coffee down in front of him. Once when he came to our house to do some remodeling work, John told me an interesting story about his dogs.

John and his wife Susan had two black Labrador Retrievers. One of the Labs died and the surviving one, Chester, hadn't been the same since. When John and Susan returned to the house after being out, Chester would always be exhausted. He'd slump quietly, lethargically into a corner or plop down onto his favorite pillow and lie there all evening, sleepy and disinterested, regardless of how much attention they gave him or what they tried to do to engage him.

After weeks of this behavior, John and Susan decided to add a puppy to their family to see if that would re-energize Chester. That's when Daisy entered the scene: a Boxer full of love and life and playfulness. Chester seemed irritated at first, but then he and Daisy became fast buddies. When they were all together – John, Susan, and the dogs – Chester and Daisy seemed happy. But when Susan left the two dogs alone in the house together, Daisy got into a lot of mischief, destroying furniture and tearing up things.

Susan was a teacher and loved her work. She had a natural nurturing personality, which she shared generously with her family and the dogs. But after a summer of being home, Susan had to return to her teaching job and begin taking care of her students, so she couldn't be home with her beloved pets as much as she would have liked. During the day she put Daisy in the basement and left Chester upstairs, thinking that would solve the problem of Daisy's mischievousness, but that didn't quite solve the problem. Daisy's antics continued in the basement.

They finally decided to hire a dog trainer to help them figure out what was going on. The trainer suggested they put a video camera in the basement during the day so they could track what was going on with Daisy. John and Susan were skeptical at first, but they were so concerned about the dogs that they agreed to give it a try.

The video footage proved revealing. It showed Daisy searching, pacing, nervously barking, and looking up (for her buddy). John and Susan knew immediately what was wrong. Daisy was searching for Chester.

The trainer suggested that Daisy was suffering from separation anxiety, so he recommended that John and Susan give her a job to do to distract her from what had become a habit she couldn't break on her own. Susan, always up for a challenge, bought Daisy a plastic ball that when rolled the right way dropped out a treat. The ball was designed to give up its treat only after a struggle, so that it wouldn't be too easy for Daisy.

Daisy ignored the ball at first, but eventually her canine curiosity took over, and she began wrestling with it. Soon after that initial interest, Daisy was hooked, and she started giving the toy her attention during the day, rather than relentlessly barking. Over time, John and Susan put Chester and Daisy in the basement together when they would go out of the house. The dogs have plenty of toys to chew on and don't do anything destructive.

Now when John comes over and I hand him a cup of coffee, he's full of good news about Chester and Daisy. John says that now, with this new job to challenge Daisy, as well as the companionship Chester and Daisy both have, the dogs are far more relaxed and much happier, and he and Susan are a lot happier, too, because they don't have to worry so much about the family dogs.

John's story reminded me that people also need to perform jobs that reward them emotionally, but that's something often much easier said than done. Today's business environment isn't designed for the personal satisfaction of its workforce; it's designed for businesses to make money. However, that doesn't mean you can't find good jobs with emotional rewards. Much like John and Susan had with Chester, you need to have a plan to make it happen. And sometimes, as you'll see in the following story about Bruce and Stu, it may take a little help from your friends.

Plans and the People Who Implement Them

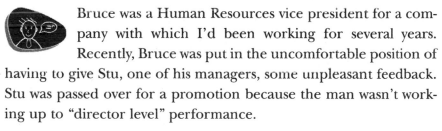 Bruce was a Human Resources vice president for a company with which I'd been working for several years. Recently, Bruce was put in the uncomfortable position of having to give Stu, one of his managers, some unpleasant feedback. Stu was passed over for a promotion because the man wasn't working up to "director level" performance.

After their talk, Bruce suggested Stuart call me to put together a plan for addressing these issues in a positive way, in hopes of turning things around.

Stu called me right away and we scheduled a time to meet once, and then to get together with Bruce. I've rarely met a nicer guy than Stu. He is a straight shooter and pulls no punches. He originally trained in finance and then switched career directions. He liked the people side of the business more than crunching numbers.

"I don't have a big ego or big career plans," Stu said at our first meeting. "I'm not aiming for Bruce's job or anything. I enjoy time with my family and want to work a reasonable number of hours. I coach Little League, too, and that's a priority. I guess I haven't been living up to Bruce's expectations. Over the last few months I've been getting signals from him that I'm not doing something right, but I'm not completely sure what it is. You know, I'm a former accounting guy, and maybe I'm too tactical for him."

"What makes you say that?" I asked Stu. He furrowed his brow, looking very much like a numbers man whose spreadsheet wasn't adding up.

"Well, because I always look at the details of everything before I can see the big picture, if I *can* get to the big picture. I'm cautious, too, so I look at problems before I look at possibilities. That drives Bruce crazy. He's a 'big idea' guy, and maybe I come across like a wet blanket."

It was a warm spring day, and we had decided to sit outside in the park. We both bought hot dogs and soda from a street vendor and settled in at a picnic table under the trees.

"You mentioned that you don't have big career plans. Do you want to become a director?"

"Yes, I do," he said. "It's not as if I don't have any ambition, but I've got to figure out how to be a bit more strategic."

"It sounds like Bruce is looking for a new level of performance from you. Why don't we get some guidance from him on exactly what he's looking for from a director-level position? We can ask him any questions we need for clarification, and then we'll put together a plan."

We finished lunch on a high note, and when we went back to my office, we scheduled a session for Stu and Bruce to meet with me.

It took place a few weeks later. Bruce and Stu came to my office together – a good sign. They sat talking with each other in the waiting area for a few minutes until I finished another appointment. They seemed at ease with one another, more like old pals than two men who had clashed at work.

"Here's the deal," Bruce began once we got behind closed doors. "Stu has been in this position for five years, and by all accounts he should be ready to move up to a director-level job. I like him a heck of a lot. We're buddies. We talk about everything that goes on, sometimes too much. But the company's growing and so is my job. I need Stu to get out of the weeds and into the boat with me."

"Tell Stu what you mean by getting out of the weeds and into the boat," I suggested.

Bruce loosened his tie and looked just a little frustrated. I'd always known him to be a patient man, but it was clear he didn't like being misunderstood, or maybe having to explain himself.

"Stu, buddy, every time I want to try something new, you tell me why we can't do it. It takes me a lot of time to convince you it'll be all right. You eventually come around, but man, it's hard work. When I ask you to take care of something, I have to follow up to make sure it's done. You've missed a couple of deadlines, and I don't think I should have to chase you down on this stuff."

I was really pleased with Bruce's candor. He wasn't trying to avoid any issues or spare Stu's feelings. I was impressed with the trust level between these two men.

"You're right," Stu replied. "Those things have happened. I do worry about the details and I get caught up in them. I'm not great at delegating, so I tend to hold onto too many projects myself. That slows me down and forces me to miss deadlines."

I wanted to keep their momentum going, so I said, "Bruce, tell Stu exactly what he needs to do if he wants to become a director. Focus on the top two-to-three things."

"OK. For starters, you need to get your department in shape and put systems in place to efficiently support on-time and accurate department reports. Then, you need to delegate work to your people so you can spend your time doing more planning and working on strategic projects with me.

"Also, I want you to brush up on your presentation skills. You'll need them for interacting more with senior management. Be more in the know of what's going on in your area. And one last thing: don't get involved in all the details."

I looked up from my note-taking and turned to Stu. He had been listening and taking notes, too. I searched for signs of defensiveness in Stu. It's not at all unusual for people to take criticism like that personally. A session could go downhill fast if that happened. But Stu seemed pretty solid. He was sitting up straight, and his body language was alert and positive.

"I think I've got what you're trying to say. I know I can do these things, but it'll be a real change for me."

"What will you need from Bruce to help you make these changes?" I asked.

"I'm not sure. When Bruce wants things done, he wants everything done yesterday."

"So how do you prioritize his requests?" I asked.

"Well, that's just it – I don't. I try to get them all done, but I can't keep up; the requests just keep coming, and I end up crashing," Stu said.

"Bruce, once Stu and I get a plan together, would you be willing to do some priority-setting with him?"

Bruce didn't even have to think about it. "Sure," he said, smiling and very enthusiastic. I could tell that he wanted this to work out as much as Stu did.

Stu and I met again the following week to begin to tackle the issues Bruce had laid out. We reviewed Bruce's concerns and added some of our own. We figured out that Stu was spending his time most days doing the following:

- 60 percent working on projects.

- 25 percent managing his department.

- 10 percent developing his people.

- 5 percent on planning and strategy.

Then we determined how Stu <u>should</u> be spending his time as a director:

- 35 percent managing his department.

- 25 percent on planning and strategy.

- 25 percent developing his people.

- 15 percent working on projects.

We immediately went to work on a plan to attack the issues that Stu knew were holding him back. It wasn't easy. Habits resist change with a vengeance. Stu discovered that his accounting training, while helpful in earlier stages of his career, was now a problem. He needed to put some of that behind him, and in doing so, developed some good insights into himself and his work:

1. A perfectionist at heart, he couldn't put a report or project down until it was 110-percent right.

2. He couldn't give a supportive opinion without having spent hours poring over the facts and figures himself.

3. He hadn't developed his people to a level where he had confidence in their abilities.

4. He wasn't developing himself, going to HR conferences, or reading broadly because he was spending most of his time on day-to-day issues.

5. He wasn't trying to spend time with other directors and senior management because he wasn't confident that he could hold his own in strategic conversations, and he felt awkward.

6. Stu even avoided Bruce at times because he didn't want to disappoint him or hear that he'd missed another deadline.

It's important to remember that plans are only as good as the people who implement them. And Stu is among the best. Benjamin Franklin is often quoted as saying, "Energy and persistence conquer all things." Stu, I believe, is the embodiment of that statement. He has spent the last ten months working on himself and his plan.

We've met with Bruce several times to check in and see how he thinks Stu is doing. Bruce is seeing a lot of improvement, and I've noticed his frustration level ebbing. At our last meeting he commented that Stu has delivered his monthly reports on time for six months in a row, that he sees Stu reaching out to other directors more, and that he and Stu are having good conversations about the future.

There's more work ahead for Stu, but he's up to the task. Now that he has a plan to guide him, some successes under his belt, and more honest communications with Bruce, I'm betting on Stu's promotion the next time it comes up.

Bruce made some great changes, too. He set clearer priorities for Stu, spent much time coaching Stu on new skills, and started giving Stu more frequent feedback along the way. Stu's skills developed, and Bruce became a more effective mentor. It turned out to be a powerful combination for raising their productivity and effectiveness. They've become a great example to the rest of the company of how to work together toward success.

High-Gain Insights

 A plan is the mechanism for turning an idea into reality. It's your commitment to yourself and a way to hold yourself accountable for the outcome. Make a plan that outlines what's important to you personally and professionally. Make sure it includes specifics about what you want to achieve and in what time frame. Be honest with yourself.

Your ability to know what you deeply desire, and to envision a future where it becomes a reality, will give you a foundation and a focus to your life. To move from concept to reality requires a plan and a series of steps, each one clear and achievable.

Big goals usually require more steps. Small goals, although they might be very important, may be achieved in a single step. One decision may create a reality. For example, "I've always wanted to travel to Europe!" might lead to you hopping online and booking a ticket and a hotel travel package.

Here are some Practical Ideas that might help you focus:

Make a plan that outlines what is important to you personally and professionally. Make sure it includes what you want to achieve and in what time frame. Be completely honest with yourself. Share the plan with your spouse, your mentor, your boss, or a trusted colleague. Enlist the aid of people to help you achieve your goals. Include:

1. Your passions.

2. Your personal goals. (family, financial, quality of life, volunteering, etc.)

3. Your career goals.

4. Your top talents, strengths, and weaknesses.

5. Skills you most need to improve.

Ask yourself the following questions to help you outline a Professional Development Plan that's right for you:

1. What are your professional goals? (For example, "I want to move up to become a senior supervisor of my department.")

2. What are the areas you need to focus on to reach those goals?

   • Do you have the personal skills to achieve your goals (such as time management, ambition, or the motivation to get results)?

   • Do you have the necessary leadership qualities to achieve your goals (such as big-picture thinking, risk-taking, project management, courage)?

     – Do you need to demonstrate that you can manage difficult people?

     – Do need to gain more experience with current technology, such as computers and software for tracking production?

   • What talents/strengths of yours will assist you in reaching your goals?

     – Are you a quick learner?

     – Are you persistent and fully committed?

     – Do you need more organizational skills?

3. What barriers to your professional development might you encounter? (From others? From yourself?)

   • Do you need an advocate to support your promotion?

   • Do you need to off-load some commitments to make time for professional development?

4. How will you achieve your goals and enhance your development? What will you do differently? Who will you enlist to help you reach new levels of success?

   • Will you be more assertive with your supervisors? (You'll need to let your bosses know your goals and what you'll need to get there. You might also want to be more assertive about your accomplishments. Don't be afraid to blow your own horn when it's appropriate.)

Are you fully committed to this plan and willing to measure your progress? Be honest!

Take this opportunity to outline a Professional Development Plan of your own:

1. What are your professional goals?

_____

_____

_____

2. What are the areas you need to focus on to reach those goals?

_____

_____

_____

3. What talents/strengths of yours will assist you in reaching your goals?

_____

_____

_____

4. What barriers to your professional development might you encounter? (From others? From yourself?)

_____

_____

_____

5. How will you achieve your goals and enhance your development? What will you do differently? Who will you enlist to help you reach new levels of success?

_____

_____

_____

Finally, remember to create a plan that you are passionate about. Examine your desires. This is a very important step, often overlooked. The great poet Ralph Waldo Emerson once said, "Every great achievement is the victory of a flaming heart."

"Take the pains required to become what you want to become or you might end up becoming something you'd rather not be."
                                                            – DONALD TRUMP

"You can't just sit there and wait for people to give you that golden dream; you've got to get out there and make it happen for yourself."
                                                            – DIANA ROSS

CHAPTER 4

Align Your Role with Your Top Talents

Scout sings.

But he shouldn't do it professionally.

Allow me to explain.

Outside of the usual barking at other dogs, passersby, and the occasional TV dog, we discovered that Scout has another talent: he's a crooner.

Last summer we had a dinner party at our home on a Friday night to celebrate our son's bar mitzvah. With twenty-five people crowded into the dining room, we proceeded to light the Sabbath candles, a weekly tradition in some Jewish households to welcome in the Sabbath. As our group of family and friends began to chant the prayers, we heard a new voice in the mix.

Scout chimed in with full, passionate howls at the top of his lungs, not quite in tune, but loud enough to make an impression on everyone at the party. I wouldn't go as far to say that Scout has any real talent for it, but it's a newly displayed skill, and that alone can be a mighty exciting experience, as I'm sure you know.

Scout has other talents too. He is an incomparable sleeper and excels at urinating on mailboxes in the neighborhood. He greets us with kisses and excitement no matter how short or long a time we have been out of the house. He snacks like a champ.

But Scout's top talents are his ever-jubilant demeanor, his effortless giving and receiving of affection, and his ability to learn. Scout's ability to learn (also a prized characteristic among human beings known as "learning agility") is so evident in his quick response to training and feedback that it almost makes me think he's gifted.

When I taught Scout the "down" command, for example, he worked hard at getting it right. We practiced this about half a dozen times until Scout nailed it. I would tell him to stay, and then I'd walk across the room. Then I'd tell him to come and, with a treat in my hand at the level of his nose, I'd say, "Down!" and move my hand to the floor. Scout learned to drop into a fully flat position and stay there until I told him it was alright for him to get up.

Well, OK, so this doesn't exactly make him Einstein, but it does show you how far a doggie treat and a little enthusiasm will go. If there is excitement, incentive, and positive reinforcement, the learning will come quicker and easier than it will with fear, intimidation, and negative reinforcement.

Everyone Has Talent

 For many of us humans, discovering our talents isn't always as easy as it was for Scout with his singing. Having other people recognize our talents can be even more of a challenge. Beth's situation is a perfect example. She had always been a well-rounded person, kind of a Renaissance woman who enjoyed going to symphony concerts, local theater productions, art films, and the museum. She prided herself on being open-minded, tolerant, and a good listener. She wanted to please people, a fine quality, but for Beth this sometimes made it difficult for her to accept criticism.

Beth seemed unusually agitated when she came to see me for one of our regularly scheduled coaching sessions.

"What's going on?" I asked.

"My boss just shared my leadership assessment with me, and I've learned that my peers don't think I'm doing a very good job as Manager of Information Technology," Beth said. I could hear the tightness in her voice, and she had a fearful look in her eyes that both people and dogs get when they're on uncertain footing.

"I'm worried," she said. "I've been in this job for fifteen years, and I don't think it's fair to be judged so harshly. After all, Colleen raised her expectations of me in this position, and I can't change overnight."

Colleen was Beth's boss. She was a tough lady who held high expectations for everyone on her team.

"I know it's upsetting to get difficult feedback," I said. "Let's take another look at the issues and see if we can understand them better. Then you can decide what you want to do and how to have a productive conversation with your boss."

I took my time fishing around in my desk for a pen. I do this when I want to give a client time to settle down and think for a few moments. My office has high, arched brick ceilings, and occasionally people get lost in thought looking up at the architecture. This is exactly what Beth was doing.

Finally she said, "OK, I'll do whatever is right for the organization, but I have to believe in the problem and the solution."

I proceeded to draw a circle on a piece of paper. I asked Beth to write three levels of information on the circle in a pie-chart format.

I told her to first identify her top three-to-four talents, the things she loves doing most of all at work, the things she is passionate about, and the things she does best. Second, I asked her to identify the major components of the job her boss was now expecting of her and the percentage of time each would take. Third, I wanted to know what percentage of her top talents would be used in each component of the new job.

Beth finished drawing the pie chart. She sat back and looked shocked. She wasn't looking up at the architecture anymore; she was completely focused on the chart.

"I'm really out of whack with this new role," she admitted. "My top talents are going to be used only 30 percent of the time in the new job. And 60 percent of the job requires leadership and strategic skills, which are my weaknesses. I guess I didn't realize how big of a gap there was. No wonder my peers are unhappy with me. I haven't been giving them what they need."

Beth looked disappointed. She held the piece of paper out in front of her cautiously, as if it were an arrest warrant. I didn't want her to lose hope. The chart was meant to illuminate, not discourage.

"It's pretty clear that the new role is not going to play to your top talents," I said, "but you have a couple of options. You could develop skills in the new areas if you're motivated to do so. Even if leadership and strategy aren't your top talents, you could make improvements in those areas, and you could fight to stay in the position.

"Or you could see if there's another position that does play to your strengths, and you could try to work that out with Colleen. Either way, you should have a conversation with Colleen soon."

This didn't exactly bring a smile to her face. There was a deeper fear lurking under her skin.

"One thing you should know..." Beth said, "I really need to keep working. I'm not financially secure right now. I'm feeling a bit at risk, and I'm not sure what's going to happen. I trust Colleen to do the right thing, but she has limits too. We all have limits, right? I can't afford to lose this job."

"OK, I understand your worries. They're legitimate. But you still have to decide what you want to do and how you want to proceed with Colleen. This doesn't have to be a negative situation. Confronting a problem is always a positive step, and I'm willing to bet Colleen will see it that way."

We sat quietly for a moment. I could see how nervous Beth was getting just thinking about what was out in front of her. She was looking up at my ceiling again.

"Look," I said, "you don't have to do it alone. I can be there with the two of you. Let me talk to Colleen, and I'll see if the three of us can meet together."

That seemed to cheer Beth up a little. All I could do was hope that Colleen would agree, and that the three of us could work out a solution to make them both happy.

Beth, Colleen, and I met a couple of weeks later. I began the meeting by establishing some ground rules. I suggested that they agree to confidentiality, to address each other with mutual respect, to listen to each other well before responding, and that they open their minds to creative solutions that might help solve any problems that arose.

Colleen's personality was the opposite of Beth's. She was a results-oriented leader who didn't give too much credence to what people thought of her as long as the job was getting done. Although this normally might create some difficulties in a sticky situation, I had high hopes for the meeting because Colleen was direct and honest and I knew she needed Beth.

Colleen began, "Beth, you're very valuable to me, and I want you to continue to contribute to the company. I know the feedback must be hard to take, but I can't imagine how we could meet our team goals without you."

I could see Beth relax a bit as she listened to what could only have sounded like very reassuring words, but then she tensed up as it was coming closer to her turn to speak.

Beth showed Colleen the pie chart we had worked on.

When Colleen saw the gaps between what the new position required and Beth's talents, she turned to Beth and said, "I see why you have been struggling over the last few months. I guess deep down I knew that the new expectations were a stretch, but I didn't realize how far of a stretch."

"What do you want to do, Beth?" I asked. "Do you want to work on the areas in which you'll need to grow?"

"I've been giving this a lot of thought, Colleen," Beth said. "I could make the improvements I'd need to succeed in the new job, but they'd never be talents. I'll work hard at it if that's what you want me to do, but I'm not sure I'll ever really love it. The truth is, I would rather focus on the technical areas I'm good at."

"What are the options available to Beth?" I asked Colleen.

"Well," Colleen replied. "I think we could have Beth focus on key projects and stay on with the department, reporting to me. She's too valuable to lose, and certainly we have plenty to keep her busy. That would mean I'd have to bring in someone else for the IT manager's role."

"What does that mean for Beth financially?" I asked, knowing Beth probably wouldn't have the courage to ask it herself.

"I can try to keep your salary and grade at the same level. I can't guarantee that, of course, but I'll talk to the Human Resources department about it. Would you be willing to make the change either way?"

"I'm OK with it," Beth said. "I think it's the right thing for the company, and I'm willing to make the change, but it won't be easy. I'm involved in a lot of ongoing projects right now, and at least two major ones I'd like to see through. But I do have a request: I want to tell my team about the change on my own terms."

"I have no problem with that," Colleen assured Beth. "Let's get together to work out the details."

Colleen and Beth both seemed to relax a bit. Sometimes during a session it's hard to tell who feels more awkward, the person getting uncomfortable feedback or the person giving it. Clearly, both these women were relieved that they'd been able to work it out.

"Thanks for taking the leadership assessment," Colleen said. "It takes guts to deal with this kind of feedback and be flexible enough to make changes. You made a tough situation a lot easier because of the graceful way in which you handled it."

Beth thanked Colleen for giving her a chance with another position and added, "I've got a lot of good working years ahead of me. I want them to be meaningful."

I was impressed with both of them for handling what could have been a very difficult situation with level heads and a focus on solutions. It took Colleen six months to fill Beth's IT spot, which gave Beth no end of satisfaction in knowing she wasn't so easy to replace after all.

Identify Your Top Talents

 You have choices in the work you do and the roles you take on. If you know what you are good at, what skills you need to work toward, and what talents you have and are passionate about, you can make better choices in your career. (Skills can sometimes masquerade as talents, but deep down, you need to know what comes naturally.)

Work hard to get yourself into a position at work where you can use your top talents 70 to 80 percent of the time. When you are in a well-aligned role, your job performance and job satisfaction increase, making you and your employer happier.

You especially need to have an accurate understanding of your talents, skills, and weaknesses when you supervise others so you create a complementary set of skills and talents on your team. You also need to understand the skills and talents of others, so you can help others better align their roles and help them develop their skills.

High-Gain Insights

 My business partner – Jim Ramerman – and I created an instrument for helping people identify their top talents. It's called the Most Natural Talent^{SM} process. It's easy to use, fun, and validates the things we do best. Here's how it works:

Choose at least ten people who know you well, either at work or outside of work. E-mail them a few questions about how they experience you at your best and how you have made an impact on them. It will take them only about five to ten minutes, tops, to respond.

Lay out all the responses you receive side by side. Read them over several times until you really understand the patterns and themes of the messages they are sending. Don't filter or interpret the messages too much, just take them in at face value. Once you think you understand the meaning, write out your most natural talents in two to three sentences. The following are some examples of Most Natural Talent^{SM} statements.

PATTI P.: *My most natural talent is strong people skills – initiating and developing relationships easily, and motivating people to achieve more. I engage others effortlessly; they open up and trust me early on. People are drawn to my positive, enthusiastic attitude and passion, and find it motivating. I have the ability to rally people around a common goal and inspire them to persist until it is achieved.*

MIKE L.: *I am perceptive and adept at getting to the real issues. I enjoy development and pursuit of strategic initiatives. I have the ability to process information quickly to formulate strategies and make decisions.*

MICHELLE P.: *I am enthusiastic, optimistic, and approachable. I am eager to bring out the best in others and help them work through their challenges. I encourage others to focus on the things that they can control and change, and to celebrate their accomplishments. My talents include diffusing difficult situations, remaining calm under pressure, looking at the big picture, and putting people at ease. I am the most effective when I am focused, have a deadline, and believe in my work.*

ANONYMOUS: *I am able to break down and analyze complex problems quickly and efficiently. People come to me for technical assistance, which is most useful at the beginning of a project.*

Now that you've completed your Most Natural Talent statement, think about your current job and ask yourself the following questions:

1. How often do I use my most natural talents in my current job? (25 percent of the time? 50 percent? 75 percent?)

2. What other major categories of skills are required in my current position? What percentage of the job are they? How good am I at them?

3. How effective am I in my current role? Why or why not?

4. How happy am I in my current role? Why or why not?

5. Is my current role aligned with my top talents?

6. What other position inside or outside of the company would be best aligned with my most natural talents?

7. What would I have to do to get the job that plays to my top talents?

8. Draw a talent/job pie chart. Here's an example of a practical idea:

Most natural talents I have	Percentage of most natural talents I'm using now	Percentage of most natural talents I'd like to be using
A. Working with clients/customers face-to-face, one-on-one.	40%	60%
B. Creating new services for clients/customers.	5%	15%
C. Working with peers in other departments to ensure high levels of customer service and implement the new services.	0%	10%

9. Pick one of your talents and come up with a plan to increase your percentage of time spent using that talent. For example, if you want to spend more time on "B," creating new services for clients/customers:

Plan these steps:

1. Delegate four hours a week of current tasks to others on my team.

2. Go to a conference where the latest ideas are presented.

3. Select the best ideas that align with my talents and adapt them to my organization.

4. Work on getting my organization to "buy in" to at least one idea and offer it to clients/customers or colleagues.

Remember that playing to your talents may go a long way toward making you a valuable employee at every level of your career.

John Wooden, the great college basketball coach who led the UCLA Bruins to several National Championships, once said, "I'd rather have a lot of talent and a little experience than a lot of experience and a little talent."

There is no substitute for talent.

CHAPTER 5
Choose Your Boss

If you have ever owned a dog, ask yourself this question: Did you choose your dog, or did your dog choose you? I've asked several people. After some reflection, they all concluded that the dog had a good bit of say in the choosing.

The whole idea of dogs choosing their owners got me thinking about the importance of people choosing their bosses. After all, you're going to spend a lot of time with your boss. That person will lead you and guide you through the day-to-day activity of your work. That person holds power and influence over you. It would certainly be to your advantage if, to ensure a good fit, you had some input into choosing your own boss.

So many clients have told me over the years how their relationships with their bosses could make or break their jobs, impact their satisfaction, and shape their ultimate success. A healthy relationship with your boss can mean happiness at work.

Is it really possible to make an informed choice about your job? About the company you want to work for and the people with whom you want to work? After all, you will probably get only a cursory introduction to the key people in your prospective organization during the interview process. Also, when you're trying to get hired, you will undoubtedly focus on things like the specifics of the job, your employer's expectations, and your benefits and compensation packages, not to mention just trying to make a good first impression. And when it's all over, it may be hard to remember much of what was said, and who said it. This doesn't leave you much time or space for choice.

Furthermore, you'll look at other career moves within the organization once you've been working for a company for a while. Most of these will probably be based as much on availability – what just happens to come along when you're looking – as on the jobs themselves and how well they fit you and your aspirations.

That's all fine. But you also need to think about the importance of choosing your boss. There are some bosses you'll get along with better than others. Some bosses have qualities that will help you meet your goals better than others. And some bosses will teach you more than others. What too many people often discover after they've accepted a position is that it's just as important, if not more so, to find the right boss as it is to find the right job.

In this chapter, you'll read about two dogs who had a good bit to do with choosing their owners and the magical relationships they formed. Then you'll hear from three people who chose their bosses, and the positive work experiences they had. My goal is to help you realize you have important choices you can make about the people for whom you work, if you're conscious and thoughtful and believe that you can.

Kayla's Choice

 My friend BJ had always loved dogs and wanted to have one from the time she was a child. This love continued after her marriage, but her husband was allergic to dogs, so she didn't push for one. Eventually BJ divorced, and she felt it was time to fulfill her childhood dream and get the dog she had always wanted.

BJ's first dog was the last of a litter of ten. There was only one dog left by the time she found the breeder. Here's how BJ describes meeting Kayla, a twelve-week-old Labrador:

"The breeder said she had only one dog left in the litter. She said the dog was terrific, but for some reason, wouldn't go to two other folks who had come to see her. For that reason, the breeder wouldn't let them have Kayla.

"But when Kayla saw me, it was like magic. She just ran to me. I honestly believe she waited for me because we were each other's guardian angels, and the universe conspired and decided we needed to come together at that moment. Corny, I know, but I swear Kayla knew I needed her as much as she needed me."

That was a defining moment for BJ in many different ways. She had always been a passionate person, but her divorce had catalyzed her to pursue her dreams. On that day, BJ rediscovered her gift. She has since transformed her love of dogs into an important avocation. Now she havens abandoned dogs right in her home, sheltering dogs that might have been put to sleep if not for BJ and other volunteers like her who take them in. She rehabilitates the dogs and readies them for adoption. She has rehabilitated seven dogs over the last five years.

Every dog that BJ has taken care of has been adopted – a remarkable record – and BJ keeps in touch with all of their adoptive families. Kayla is head of the pack, of course, and helps keep the other dogs in line. Kayla's nephew Cody also helps, as does Spirit, a Husky who has joined BJ's family.

BJ will pop up again later in the book, but I wanted to introduce her briefly here to set up Milo's story.

Milo's Choice

 Milo was one of the dogs BJ took in. He escaped one night through the fence in BJ's yard. Milo trotted down the street and appeared several blocks away at the glass door of my friends Alice and Steve. One house to the left or to the right, and Milo's life would have taken a different course. Steve and Alice didn't know BJ at the time, but Milo was about to change all of that.

Inquisitive, wandering, probably a bit frightened, Milo stared at Steve through the glass door until Steve finally noticed him. Milo had big brown eyes and an innocent look. Steve opened the door and welcomed Milo in.

Here is how Steve described it:

"Alice, my wife, was unhappy about letting a dog in the house. She was crystal clear about not wanting to add a dog into our mix of four cats. But she was willing to let Milo stay so we could keep him safe until we found his owner. If you ever get lost, you want Alice to help you. She's great in a crisis – very resourceful and level-headed."

"We have an enclosed mudroom on the other side of that glass door. Letting the dog into the mudroom seemed innocent enough to both of us. He was safe, but neither one of us embraced him right away. We made two phone calls – one to the number on his tag and the other to Animal Control. As we planned, Animal Control picked up Milo so he would be sheltered until his owner reclaimed him."

"There were some early signs that fate was taking control. The first sign was that the dog didn't bark. We liked that. He sat sweetly alone in the mudroom while we sorted things out. Accelerating the erosion of our resolve, he seemed to like being with us. With his tail wagging, Milo left with Animal Control to continue his adventure."

"That was when the story began getting complicated. The Animal Service League called us and asked us to take Milo back 'for a short time.' They told us Milo lived just down the street in BJ's shelter, but BJ couldn't come out to get Milo, and would we mind dog-sitting just for a little while."

"I didn't even know BJ at the time. We've since become great friends. We have Milo to thank for that. Anyway, I said yes, and this time, when Alice wasn't paying attention, I let Milo out of the mud-room and into the house. When I finally got around to walking Milo back to BJ's shelter just a few houses away, something magical happened. I had already gotten attached to Milo, and as we walked together down the street, I realized I wanted to make Milo a part of our home."

"It was instantaneous. It just hit me. I knew that Milo had picked me out of a lineup, and it was meant to be. I knew I'd have to really sell Alice on it, but I just couldn't let Milo go."

"It has been five years since that walk down the street. Milo has changed our lives in positive ways. He's made my wife a dog person. He brought BJ into our lives, and she has become an extended member of our family. He makes us laugh and has re-taught us how to play and have fun. We are so grateful Milo chose to come to our house that night, and that we allowed ourselves to be chosen."

Is It Time to Change Your Boss?

 Regardless of whether you believe that Kayla and Milo were savvy enough to pick their owners, you'll probably agree that it would be nice if, from time to time, you could be as intuitive as your favorite dog. The intuition that we often see in animals is a survival skill that many of us humans have either lost or never fully developed. But intuition often presents itself to us in the form of inspiration. Patrick's story is a great example of this.

Patrick had been working for his boss, Jill, for almost two years. Jordan, the manager of the department, had brought in Jill to boost the department's credibility and performance. Patrick participated in the interview process for recruiting his new boss. Unfortunately,

Jill wasn't his first choice, and ultimately, it was Jordan's decision to make.

Things weren't great between Patrick and Jill right from the start. Patrick had been close to Jill's predecessor, a well-respected company leader. Patrick held Jill to a standard that, in all likelihood, was probably too high for anyone. And Patrick, although he wouldn't admit it, had always been a bit resistant to change. He came from a hard-working, blue-collar family. His father had been a bricklayer and a member of the union for more than thirty years before he retired. His mother had raised four boys on her own while her husband was out working. Patrick can remember that from the time he was a little boy, everyone in the family had a job to do each day like clockwork. Whether it was taking out the garbage, cutting the lawn, cleaning the bathroom, or changing all the bed sheets, you either did it or gave up your portion of mashed potatoes or your treasured scoop of chocolate pudding.

It didn't help that Jill was younger, somewhat privileged, and had graduated from what Patrick called "a college with a reputation." She wasn't a great team-builder and didn't give much in the way of encouraging feedback, which was bothersome for a man who had grown up in a tight-knit, supportive family. In fact, Patrick only heard from Jill when there was a problem, which in Patrick's case, was turning out to be true more and more frequently.

Patrick was a strong performer who had always received glowing reviews and raises. He was growing increasingly frustrated with Jill, with his own job, and with the company. In spite of his efforts, he was dreading going to meetings with Jill. His one-on-one meetings with her, which happened infrequently, often turned into sessions on what he was doing wrong or could be doing better. For the first time in a twenty-year career, Patrick was thinking about leaving the company.

Patrick and I had worked together on his leadership skills for several years. He had received a promotion and had successfully changed leadership roles twice. His career had been on an upward trajectory until Jill arrived. Now it looked as if things might derail.

Patrick was spending an increasing amount of time grumbling about Jill at our sessions. At first, he tried different strategies in working with her, and this was productive. But none of them seemed to stick, and Patrick was growing disheartened.

Then, one day, Patrick came in with an interesting idea. A new position had opened up in a different division. The man running the division, Don, had a great reputation as a leader. What if Patrick tried to get a transfer to work for him?

"What a great idea," I said.

"There's one catch," Patrick said. "I'd have to take a step down in position to work for him. The job openings in his division aren't at my level."

"Interesting situation. Let's lay out a plan for what you're seeking, and the pros and cons of staying or going. Then you can make up your mind."

Patrick determined that he was looking for five characteristics in a boss:

1. Someone he could trust and someone who trusted him.

2. Someone he respected and someone who respected him.

3. Someone who gave him clear and measurable goals.

4. Someone who believed in developing a strong team mentality.

5. Someone who believed in helping him grow, was a good coach, and invested in his development.

Then Patrick wrote down the following information, with all the details filled in:

1. His personal goals.

2. His career goals.

3. His top talents.

4. Skills he needed to improve.

5. Jill's business goals and objectives.

6. Jill's leadership strengths and weaknesses.

If he were to pursue the new position, Patrick felt it was important to interview with Don in a new way. He would have to be able to determine whether Don was the kind of person for whom he wanted to work while Don was trying to figure out if Patrick was the kind of person he wanted on his team.

Patrick and I worked together to create a series of questions he would ask Don. We built a plan for talking to other people in Don's division about what it was like to work for him. Patrick also went to a friend in the Human Resources department for her input and guidance.

Patrick talked it over with his wife to see whether they could make a lifestyle change to offset a pay decrease. On the upside, he also promised to negotiate somewhat more manageable working hours and less travel time away from home. His wife supported his plans.

George Eliot once said, "The strongest principle of growth lies in human choice." I'm constantly aware of this whenever I work with people who face difficult choices. But if you do all the difficult prep work, as Patrick did, you lower your level of risk along with the fear of the unexpected.

Patrick got the chance he wanted and decided to take the leap. He went into his new situation with his eyes open. He felt good about his plan, and there were no surprises. Patrick made the right decision (much as Milo had when he picked Alice and Steve). Don turned out to be the kind of boss Patrick wanted. And now that he's getting home at a more reasonable hour, he and his wife and family are happier with his job, too.

Colin Goes to Washington (In His Own Words)

I had a track record of choosing positions because something about each of them evoked passion in me. Working in broadcast television for five years gave me opportunities to meet exciting, famous people. The work was deadline-driven, fast-paced, and satisfied my need to be creative.

For the next ten years, I channeled my passion for helping people into working for nonprofit and local- and state-government organizations focused on stopping the spread of HIV and serving people affected by the virus.

After several years of interesting and satisfying work at one job, there were major executive-level staff changes. All of a sudden, I found myself in an administrative position. I went from a Raging Bull to a Minnie Mouse in seconds flat. I lacked the authority to make meaningful decisions, and I was assigned mundane projects. So, after repeated unsuccessful attempts to improve my situation, I began looking for something new, something exciting and dynamic.

Thirty-eight years old and looking for another position, I struggled to come to terms with reality. I knew I might never again feel the passion or compassion that led me to work in TV journalism or to serve people with HIV.

I've worked for lots of people throughout my various careers. Some bosses were good and some were lousy. Well, maybe that's not fair. Maybe "uninspiring" would be a better word. Either way, I believed my prospects were slim for finding something that excited me, but then I found someone who did: a passionate, articulate, elected official who was a staunch protector of consumers' and civil rights, and – a rarity among Washington's political elite – an effective legislator.

Her intelligence, commitment to public service, successful track record of taking on tough issues, and experience in overcoming personal tragedy inspired me. *She* inspired me. Working for any legislator, my friends warned me, would be very unpredictable, intense, and stressful. I imagined what it would be like to work for her before I took the job, to learn from her, and gain firsthand public policy-making experience.

Some of her current and former employees said that she could be challenging to work for, but that she treated her staff better than most other elected officials did. She expected her staff to work hard, but rarely phoned them outside of regular working hours. She was not unrealistic in her demands.

While a bit afraid of working in the political arena, I was open to it. It seemed to combine the deadline-driven intensity of television with the potential for really making an impact on the lives of people as I had done in HIV services.

How would I do in such an environment? Could I live on less salary? What did I need to feel personally satisfied and professionally challenged?

I searched inside myself and found my answers. She personified what I believed I needed in a leader. She was someone whom I respected, and she respected her staff. I was excited enough about the opportunity that I was even willing to take a significant salary cut to join her team.

More than a year has passed since I accepted the position. I've learned a lot in that time. Like any boss, she has her liabilities. But believe me, her liabilities are far outweighed by her strengths. She's smarter than most people I've come across. She's a great policy-maker and a perceptive politician.

Would I decide to work for her again? You bet! I feel as if I've been paid to learn about a whole new world. I've seen firsthand what it takes to pass a bill through our country's political machinery. I've learned to hone my abilities to influence people. I've gotten visibility with legislators. But my best lesson has been that nothing beats working for someone whom you respect and who treats you with respect.

Terry Picks His Dream Boss (In His Own Words)

 Most people leave their jobs because they can't stand their bosses. I'm no exception. But up until about ten years ago, I let my bosses pick me. It never occurred to me that I had the option of picking them.

I built my corporate career by looking at potential jobs for the sake of a carefully thought-out career strategy. I defined each step in terms of long-term goals. I spent a lot of time getting ready to impress potential employers, and I worked hard to nail down the "perfect interview."

I never took the risk of being genuine. I didn't pay attention to the things that might provide a true picture of me to my potential boss. And I never took the time to really think about what it might be like to work for that person. The result was a mixed bag.

Some of the people who hired me were running businesses that were very successful from an outside perspective. But once I got inside, it became all too clear that the business and the boss were a mess. I also ran into truly inspired leaders, fun and flawed and capable of great things. And their business success reflected that.

As my responsibilities grew, my bosses grew increasingly demanding. Those demands were not a problem, but another issue kept cropping up. Some of my employers did not make it a priority to connect with me as the work took its toll, and their demands were based only on the needs of business and not my needs and limitations as a human being.

In one memorable episode, I spoke up to a boss while we worked together one Saturday morning. I pointed out that as our business grew, my weeks got longer. I had been working six long days per week for some time and desperately needed another person on my team. My response shocked me. "Talk to me," he said, "when you're coming in every Sunday."

To be fair, I had approached my job interviews positioning myself strictly as a business asset, so it really shouldn't have surprised me when I was treated that way. I offered performance, and my bosses took me at my word. This began to deeply affect my attitude toward work and myself. I continued to be successful, but was often exhausted, distracted, and sad.

Finally, I decided to try something different. I decided to look for a new boss who was skilled at leading a team of people, not a pack of wolves.

I spoke to some senior managers. I found the nerve to challenge each one of them to talk to me about what it might be like to work for them. At last I met Russell, a top leader with a great reputation in a progressive corporation.

Russell had a very rich spiritual life and a positive, supportive disposition. Everything about his personality convinced me that he would be the right leader for me.

Another nice surprise came out of all this. In addition to working for a great boss, I discovered that the other people who worked for Russell were also terrific. Not a spoiled banana in the bunch. It seems that good people have a knack for finding other good people, regardless of their backgrounds and skill levels. Russell opened my eyes once again to the joys and possibilities of work.

High-Gain Insights

 Whether you've ever been involved in choosing or being chosen by a dog, choosing the bosses for whom you want to work might become one of the most important skills you learn in your working life. When bosses begin to understand that you have a choice to work for them or someone else, they may want to focus on becoming better bosses. Everybody wins when that happens.

Furthermore, people don't leave companies, they leave people. If you want to be happier in your job, it might help if you began by more consciously choosing the person for whom you want to work, and the *culture* in which you want to work. It's a skill you can learn. And it's an empowering and career-savvy move. Earlier in this chapter, we saw how Patrick determined that he was looking for five characteristics in a boss:

1. Someone he could trust and someone who trusted him.

2. Someone he respected and someone who respected him.

3. Someone who gave him clear and measurable goals.

4. Someone who believed in developing a strong team mentality.

5. Someone who believed in helping him grow, was a good coach, and invested in his development.

What characteristics are important to you when you think about choosing a boss?

Author Leo Buscaglia once wrote, "What we call the secret of happiness is no more a secret than our willingness to choose life." Once you put your mind to it, you may be surprised at the number of choices available to you. Make an important commitment to your working life by following some Practical Ideas:

First, determine the top five most important characteristics you are looking for in a boss. Once you know the characteristics you would like in a boss, make a plan that details how you'd go about finding the person for whom you would most want to work:

1. Talk to people in your company or your prospective company about their bosses.

2. Talk to the Human Resources department.

3. Talk to people outside your company about their bosses and culture.

4. Evaluate your current boss objectively.

5. Put together a short but insight-generating set of questions (based on the characteristics) you want to ask your potential new boss. Here are some questions you might consider:

- What increases or decreases your trust in someone for whom you work?

- What increases or decreases your respect for a boss?

- How does the boss foster his/her team?

- How much time does the boss spend coaching and developing people? What level of investment do you make?

- What would the goals and objectives for the position be and how would they be measured?

Then make the bold decision to either stay with your current boss or take steps to find and move to a boss who will be a big part of supporting your success and joy at work.

"Destiny is not a matter of chance, it's a matter of choice; it's not a thing to be waited for, but a thing to be achieved."
— WILLIAM JENNINGS BRYAN

CHAPTER 6
Manage Your Emotions

My friend Sharon has two dogs. Bailey is a Black Labrador mix, a strong, friendly female. Maggie is a gentle Collie with the personality of a tentative little girl. Sharon no longer keeps the dogs in cages, or "crates." Instead they are baby-gated into the laundry room, which contains their food, water bowls, and two dog beds. To keep the beds from slipping on the wooden floor, they are placed on two inexpensive cotton area rugs.

The dogs have a safe place to stay where they won't get into trouble when the family is out of the house. It seemed like a pretty good setup. Unfortunately, Sharon had no idea what kind of trouble Bailey could find right in the laundry room.

"Bailey is most definitely the alpha dog," Sharon said. "She is deeply attached to her 'sister,' Maggie, a ten-year-old Collie. She sleeps curled around Maggie with her head resting on Maggie's chest. It's one of the most precious things you'd ever want to see. But Bailey is no angel. She steals Maggie's toys and food if no one is watching. She pushes Maggie out of the way if someone is trying to pet Maggie. And she tears past Maggie to get into the house first."

Bailey was acting strangely for about a week. She wasn't herself and seemed lethargic. Within a few days she stopped eating and then stopped drinking. Then she started vomiting. Sharon was understandably concerned and decided it was time to visit the vet.

The vet ran an X-ray and discovered that Bailey had a large mass in her intestines. It turned out that Bailey was nervous one night and ate part of the cotton rug in the laundry room. Without medical attention, she might have died. Luckily, they found the problem and fixed it before she suffered any long-term damage.

Some months later, Sharon left the dogs overnight in their room. She once again discovered that Bailey had shredded the one remaining rug. She brought Bailey to the vet immediately. This time, the vet induced vomiting, and Bailey came home later that day. There are no more rugs in their room, and she has been fine since. To this day Sharon has no idea why Bailey wanted to munch on those rugs. Was it anger, fear, insecurity? Although the vet had no clear explanation to offer, he was sure of at least one thing: Bailey was experiencing some sort of an emotional problem.

Anger Is the Tip of the Iceberg

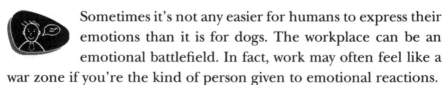 Sometimes it's not any easier for humans to express their emotions than it is for dogs. The workplace can be an emotional battlefield. In fact, work may often feel like a war zone if you're the kind of person given to emotional reactions.

Pete, a writer at an advertising agency, worked with me on a management-development program he and his coworkers went through. Pete was a big guy, tall with broad shoulders. When he entered a room, you knew it, and when he entered emotionally charged, he cut an intimidating figure.

Pete stormed into my office one afternoon for an appointment, sat down firmly in the chair, and declared, "I'm going nuts! I suddenly realize that my priorities are completely out of whack.

I'm working way too many hours to please my boss and our clients. I haven't seen my family in weeks, and my wife is getting resentful. There's no end to this."

He paused for a moment. He was just about strangling the arms of the chair.

"I blew up at Ray today."

Ray was Pete's boss.

"Couldn't help it. Second time it's happened this year. The guy is married to his work. He does anything the clients want no matter how much it stresses the rest of us out. I'm really pissed off at him."

"How about you take a deep breath and tell me about it," I said as light-heartedly as I could. I think he needed a friendly voice at that moment more than anything else.

"And go ahead, loosen the tie. I won't tell on you."

He gave in with a slight smile.

"Thanks. I know you're gonna tell me I was wrong to take it out on him, but I didn't know where else to go with all this anger. Now he's upset with me, and I guess I can't blame him. Maybe he'll fire me."

Pete blanched. He clearly didn't like the idea of getting fired. I'm not sure whether he believed that would really happen, or whether he was waiting for my reaction.

"Did Ray say he wanted to fire you?" I asked.

"No."

"Well, that's good. Let's assume Ray realizes you've been under a lot of pressure and he's going to cut you some slack. So, where are all these feelings coming from, how much of this is really about Ray, and how much is about you?"

Pete thought that through for a few moments.

"Ever since I started at the agency, Ray has made it clear I am on call pretty much 24/7. I agreed to that from the start, but that was four years ago. Every time I say 'yes' to yet another all-nighter, it only opens the door for the next time."

"When I started, I didn't have kids, but now I've got two babies. It isn't easy for my wife when I'm not there. She's pretty much on her own. I don't know how much more she'll take of this."

"So tell me more about Ray," I said.

"Ray's a long-term agency guy. He works ridiculous hours, never questions the clients, and expects us to pull all the weight. He's not a bad guy. We used to go out for drinks and hang out when we had more time. That pretty much stopped about a year ago."

"Have you tried to talk to him? I mean other than the explosions?"

That got another quick smile out of Pete.

"I haven't told him how I really feel because I know it won't matter. So I keep all this stuff bottled . . . upand then I guess it just exploded. Probably not the greatest career move, huh?"

"Probably not," I agreed. "How many of these feelings are about Ray, and how many are about you that might be directed at Ray?"

"I'm not sure I understand your question."

"Are you worn out?"

"Yes."

"Are you frustrated?"

"Yes."

"Are you losing your creative juices?"

"Yes."

"Are you scared about losing your marriage?"

"Yes."

"Are you scared you might lose your job?"

"Yes."

He was beginning to understand.

"Anger is just the tip of the iceberg," I said. "It sounds like you agreed to certain terms from the start and now you're not happy with the deal. I don't think you're as much upset with Ray as you are with yourself."

I softened my tone so he wouldn't think I was attacking him. The last thing he needed now was to take another hit.

"You're not going to have a great relationship with Ray if he has to wonder when you're going to blow up next. Your coworkers are probably aware of what's happened. How do you think this could affect your relationship with them? You're going to have to find a more effective way of managing your emotions if you want healthy relationships with your boss and coworkers and a career with the agency."

"Yeah, you're right. You're not telling me anything I don't already know."

"Also, have you ever considered that you have some choices, including changing the terms of the deal?"

"I guess that's true, but I don't know how he'd react. He's got a job to do, and if I'm not willing to do my part, he just might go out and find somebody else who is."

"Maybe," I said, "but how do you know if you don't ask? You also owe him an apology. Why don't you start with that? Then let him know what you're really worried about, and maybe your relationship with Ray and your job can be salvaged."

Pete just shook his head. But he was smiling now. There was a glimmer of hope. Maybe he could still work this out with Ray.

Pete sat down and talked with his wife over the next few weeks. They determined how much work was reasonable for him. He apologized to Ray and his coworkers, and he didn't lose his job.

Pete's still working on not letting things build up inside; that will probably be a lifelong project for him. But he had learned that confronting issues and exploring anger could actually make things better.

*   *   *

Scout is an excitable dog. It doesn't take much to get him into a heightened emotional state. When he's greeting a person he hasn't met before, he puts his front paws up on the person's legs, sniffs, and tries to lick that person's face. It might pass for cute in small dogs like Scout, but it's not. In fact, it's an act of dominance.

Bob, my dog trainer, taught me that it's best never to approach or make eye contact with a new dog. It's always better to let the dog come to you first. As I mentioned earlier, when Bob first met Scout, he never looked at or acknowledged him. He didn't pet him or touch him; consequently, Scout did not do his usual jump-up-and-bark routine. He remained in a calm, submissive state.

One night Scout came into our bedroom and made a beeline for the bedside table in the corner of the room. He squeezed underneath it, wailed, and shook in a way I haven't seen before or since. I couldn't console him. I would try to coax him out and hold him, but the only place he wanted to be was under that table.

The next day we checked with our vet, but he couldn't really tell us anything. We also checked our hidden electric-fence system. We wanted to make sure it hadn't malfunctioned and that Scout wasn't reacting to the piercing "beep" of the warning signal. The only conclusion we were able to draw was that Scout was detecting something outside of the house that scared him. We couldn't hear it or see it, but Scout sure could, and he took himself to a place he could feel safe.

Adjusting Your Behavior

 By the time Laurie started working with me, the issues in her finance group were already coming to a head. Some of her team members had complained to Human Resources about Laurie's management style. Some said they weren't sure if they wanted to stay on her team.

I conducted a leadership assessment of Laurie by talking with her direct employees, her boss, and the Human Resources manager who had referred her to me. I learned as much as I could about her management style and the dynamics within her group.

Before I give a client the results of an assessment, I try to schedule some quiet time to prepare. I steady myself and my emotions and try to put myself into that person's shoes. I'm better able to serve them when I'm calm and clear-headed.

When Laurie and I met to review the assessment, I was prepared for a range of possible responses from her, everything from anger to denial to acceptance. I never know how people will react, and rather than assume, I try to mentally prepare myself for all the possibilities.

Laurie looked a bit apprehensive, unsure of what she might hear. She knew she was receiving my help because her people had complained. That's a tough place to begin. I offered her something to drink. She requested a bottle of water, and one of our staff placed it on the table in front of her.

The assessment confirmed what Laurie already knew at some level: Her leadership of the group wasn't going well.

Laurie's team saw her as an exceptionally smart finance manager who was good with internal clients and quick to attack problems, but she was a de-motivating leader. She gave too much negative feedback and not enough encouragement. She had gotten angry a couple of times and said harsh things to people in front of others, which embarrassed them.

She blamed others when things on the team weren't done perfectly, and she didn't take responsibility for the issues. Laurie wasn't very available to review projects along the way, so by the time she looked at them, it was late in the game and work had to be redone. Lastly, she hadn't developed her people, which meant other managers weren't confident in delegating tasks to them. This was creating a bottleneck in the office and an imbalance in the workflow.

Laurie read the assessment report fully before setting it down and looking up. She put her elbows on the table, leaned forward, and rested her chin in her hands. I waited for her to speak, and when it became apparent she wouldn't, or couldn't, I knew it was going to be up to me to get things started.

"I know this can be an emotional process, and I want to give you time to think and feel. But I'm curious to know what your gut reaction is to the feedback."

"I'm not surprised by any of it, really. I guess I knew people were unhappy. But I didn't know they were *this* unhappy."

I could see that Laurie was still absorbing the feedback. And she was very, very nervous. She hadn't even touched the bottle of water she'd requested.

"What does this confirm for you? What were the surprises?"

"It confirms what I've been seeing. People on the team have pretty much stopped coming to me. The only time we've been interacting is around project deadlines. I haven't really had time to meet with the team members individually anymore. Too much work. We're all too busy."

"What surprises me is that I've somehow hurt some of them. I didn't mean for that to happen. My patience has been short on some of these projects, so I've said some pretty harsh things, I guess, but I never meant to hurt anyone. I feel awful."

Laurie was beginning to see the impact of her behavior. I decided to move ahead carefully; I wanted to keep her focused on the issues instead of the pain.

"What do you think the impact of your behavior has been on the team?" I asked.

"Well, I can't believe they have a whole lot of trust in me at this point," she said a bit nervously.

"I think you're right. But I believe it can be fixed if you're ready to take responsibility for what's happened and really connect with people. Are you up to trying to understand what may have been driving some of these emotions in you?"

"Yes. I obviously can't go on like this."

"Think of a time when you've gotten angry with someone on your team. What do you think was going on with you at that moment, underneath the anger?"

"On this one project, we were under a lot of pressure from the comptroller to get it done. He had to report to the CFO. When I gave him our preliminary numbers, he found some mistakes and got upset. He said he needed to rely on the work of my team. So I went back to the team and I guess I let some of them have it. It probably wasn't the best way to handle things, but I was just trying to get the numbers right."

"We judge ourselves by our intentions, and we judge others by their behaviors. You're being judged by your behaviors, not by your intentions. I'm thinking that when your boss was upset that the numbers weren't right, you might have been worried and upset too."

"I was," Laurie admitted.

"Do you think your worry was that you couldn't trust the team to get things right?" I asked.

"I don't think it was a matter of not trusting the team. I think they are doing things too quickly and not thoroughly. There are too many projects going on. Not enough peer reviews are taking place. I'm not spending enough time teaching them. By the time it got to my boss, it was too late. I should have caught the errors, too, but I didn't. I have really good people on my team, but we're not leveraging each other well on these projects."

"So what needs to change, starting with you?" I asked.

"I need to slow down and start spending more time with the team. I need to stop reacting so quickly to mistakes, and I need to take more responsibility for the issues, not blame others. Would that be a good place to start?" she asked.

"Yes. But I think you'll need to do a bit more than that. You've lost a lot of respect, and you'll have to regain it."

She sighed and her shoulders slumped, as if she'd taken a physical blow. The truth, as we all know, can sometimes hurt. Laurie was apprehensive.

"OK," she said. "Where do we start?"

We planned a half-day retreat with the whole team. Laurie also decided to invite her boss and the HR manager. She wanted to share her full feedback report with the team. It was a bold and courageous move and a great step in demonstrating her new level of accountability for her actions.

She started working on all the things she mentioned, and in six weeks we gathered for the retreat.

Laurie chose an off-site location to get people out of the office and onto neutral ground. The setting was a golf resort, and although it was winter, large glass windows surrounded the room letting in waves of natural light. We all dressed casually, which lent a relaxed atmosphere to the day.

Her boss, the HR manager, and her team filed in. They looked uncertain as to what was going to happen. They made small talk with each other, but their eyes kept darting to Laurie.

I imagined they were wondering how she was doing and what she might say.

I started the day in the usual way. We set confidentiality guidelines and ground rules for good participation and High-Gain conversations. I added that some of what was going to be discussed was highly sensitive information about Laurie, so we wanted to take our time and not rush. Everyone looked attentive.

Laurie readied herself to address the group. She hadn't told me ahead of time what she was going to say, although I knew she'd written down her remarks. She fixed her gaze on her notes as she started.

"As you know, I've been working on my leadership skills for the last several months, and I've gotten feedback from you on what's been going well and not so well. First, I want to thank each of you for taking the time to offer me feedback. It meant a lot to me. I hope you'll see I've taken it to heart, and I'm doing something about it."

I looked around the room watching for reactions. There weren't any yet.

She continued, "I'm going to share the feedback report with you in a minute, but before you read it, I want to apologize for some of my emotional outbursts and behaviors. I could make excuses for myself, but I won't. I was wrong and I hurt some of you. I'm truly sorry about that."

People seemed surprised and impressed. I don't think they had ever heard a manager be so honest and direct with them before.

Laurie handed out the report and everyone began to read with genuine interest.

Laurie took charge again when it was time to get the session started. She went over all the issues and told the group which ones she had decided to work on and why. They asked a couple of questions, but mostly listened.

Then Laurie looked down at her papers, and a few tears welled in her eyes. It was clear she wanted to say something important.

"You're a great team, and I don't tell you that enough. You do wonderful work. I appreciate each and every one of you."

She then went around the room, one by one, telling her people something positive and why she appreciated them. By the time she was done, there wasn't a dry eye in the room. It was one of the most remarkable sessions I'd ever seen.

When Laurie finished, her team actually applauded. There were smiles all around the table. Several people asked her if she was OK, making sure their boss was holding up alright. Laurie had broken through to them. She appreciated their acknowledgement but didn't dwell on it. She understood that real respect was earned, and she would have to continue to work hard at it. Finally, she was ready and willing to do it.

High-Gain Insights

 When you're calm and clear-headed, you perform better and make better decisions. If you want to manage your emotions, start by understanding yourself better. Determine the trigger points or hot buttons that might set you off and how your emotions impact other people. Get feedback about yourself; don't guess!

Here are some Practical Ideas that might help you get a grip on your emotions:

1. Get in touch with the most frequent and intense feelings you have at work. The following is a list of feelings to help you get started. Circle the ones that you often experience. Begin by saying, "At work, I feel . . ."

Angry	Confused	Distrusting	Frustrated	Repulsed
Anxious	Connected	Energized	Happy	Satisfied
Appreciated	Creative	Engaged	Indignant	Supported
Apprehensive	Curious	Excited	Inspired	Undermined
Bold	Depressed	Exhausted	Peaceful	Withdrawn
Bored	Disinterested	Fearful	Rejected	Worried

2. Select two feelings to explore and answer the following questions:

   • What are the real root causes of each of these feelings?

   • What part of the feeling is something that's caused by external forces (at home and/or at work)?

   • What part belongs to you (your attitude, your choices, etc.)?

3. Take steps to:

   • Deepen, or make more consistent, positive feelings by doing more of what causes those feelings.

   • Decrease or eliminate a negative feeling by taking steps to address the root cause.

Keep in mind that emotions are neither good nor bad. They are a part of our human condition, and it is the way we react to them that is important. Emotions themselves can liberate us if we understand them. The great psychologist Carl Jung said, "There can be no transforming of darkness into light, and of apathy into movement, without emotion." Emotions are part of us, and we need them to succeed.

"I know the price of success: dedication, hard work, and an unremitt-ing devotion to the things you want to see happen."
— FRANK LLOYD WRIGHT

"Manage your emotions; it makes all of the rest, or none of it, possible."
— SHERRI MCARDLE AND JIM RAMERMAN

CHAPTER 7
Get and Give More Feedback

Our dog trainer, Bob, says that you have three seconds from the time a dog takes an action until you reward him or correct his behavior; otherwise your response will have no impact. After those critical three seconds, your dog can't associate his behavior with your response.

The good news about that is I've learned to reward and correct Scout immediately in command training and on our walks. The bad news is I've never been able to catch Scout when he urinates in the house, so he hasn't gotten my "feedback" on that matter.

Learning how to give Scout feedback started with Bob giving me some. From the first time I spoke to Bob, he spoke the truth to me. He calls it the way he sees it. Direct. Unvarnished. Unapologetic. That's the kind of feedback I needed to learn to give to Scout, and few people are as knowledgeable and direct as Bob when it comes to dogs.

My husband Terry would say he's been trying to give me feedback for years about Scout (and other things), and I haven't been listening. That's probably true. It's clear that Bob is training me more than he's training Scout. Bob says dogs learn things quickly; people, on the other hand, take time.

I don't always get new techniques right the first time. For some reason, I don't get Scout's leash to pop just right or quite fast enough when I give Scout a correction. Sometimes it comes off as a tug. Sometimes it's a pop, but too late. I used to think I was fairly coordinated until Bob started giving me feedback. It's a good thing he's patient with me, and I'm learning to be more patient with myself.

Patience is not one of my virtues – just ask those who know me. I'm clear, direct, and focused. I like my feedback straight up with an encouraging tone. I like to learn something once and do it. But working with dogs is a different story.

Scout really wants to please me. During our training times at home, he is so excited by the thought of encouraging feedback and a treat that he often tries to anticipate my commands. This can lead to a bit of confusion on his part, because if he's not listening to me, he might be responding to a command I didn't give. It's pretty funny to watch him when he gets into this mode.

When we train at Lollypop Farm, where Bob works, Scout is distracted by all of the scents of the other dogs who have been in the room before us. He wanders around the room, sniffs everything, and has to be guided by me and the leash to our lesson. It's seems odd to me that Scout doesn't respond to Bob's commands or rewards directly. Even with his favorite treat in Bob's hand, Scout won't take it from Bob. For some reason, he looks to *me*. So I do all the training with Scout one-on-one, and Bob guides the two of us through it.

There are three types of feedback I've been using with Scout. The first is verbal. I encourage him with a lot of "good boy!"s when he does something right, and I reward him with a small treat. The second is physical. I poke him firmly to get his attention so he reacts immediately to my commands. The third is my emotional energy. I work on my calm, assertive leadership energy around him, especially on our walks. He knows from my energy, from the way I hold myself and the leash, that I'm in charge and he needs to follow my lead.

I learned these last two methods from Cesar Millan of *The Dog Whisperer* on the National Geographic channel, and I've found them to be very helpful.

Scout's attention span for training sessions lasts about twenty minutes – and so does mine. After that, he's tired, his focus is gone, and he's easily distracted. That's another good lesson about feedback. Do it skillfully, keep it focused, and complete it in a relatively short period of time.

Training Scout and giving him feedback is a discipline I've had to develop. It's a lot like parenting, although children and dogs need distinct kinds of leadership. Each of my children is different. Rachel, the oldest, needs clear rules, limits, and boundaries along with encouragement. She makes her best decisions when she can't negotiate her way around the issue at hand. On the other hand, Matt, our youngest, needs a lot of encouragement and to feel that as he earns our trust, he receives more responsibility and accountability for his actions.

I've had to stretch my parenting and dog-leadership skills to give them all what they need when they need it. That has required new levels of skills and agility from me. On a good day, when I'm rested and emotionally present, I get it right. On a bad day, I get more feedback that I'm not doing it so well.

I believe that feedback says more about the sender than the receiver. With Scout, I've come to realize that I get the behavior I tolerate. So, I give feedback to Scout immediately now.

Bob suggested we keep a short lead on Scout in the house for quite a few weeks in the beginning. When Scout stepped out of line, I gave him a correction. For instance, he's not allowed to go up the stairs in front of me anymore. He has to wait at the bottom of the stairs in a stay position until I reach the top. Then I give him an "OK!" command, and he can follow.

Scout's feedback to me comes in the quality and quantity of his follower behavior. When he looks to me for cues on what's acceptable and follows my commands, he is encouraged and rewarded. If I were to let him sit on my lap or to come up on the bed (which I don't anymore!), I'd be giving him signals that he's in charge and he would retake the dominating role in an instant.

Scout responds best to encouragement. That's been an important lesson for me. If I get frustrated and raise my voice or bark out a command, Scout pretty much ignores me. All he sees is a weird human who can't control her emotions. That doesn't make him confident in my leadership.

I've been working on improving my encouraging presence at home and at work, and Scout's been a good teacher. Bob says that dogs respond best to encouragement. I've found that dogs are a lot like people in that respect.

Scout also needs course corrections from me to understand his limits and boundaries and my feedback has to be pretty immediate to be effective. That keeps me on my toes with him. It's a new kind of relationship we're forging, and I like it a lot better.

Training time for Scout and me has become a crucial part of what we do together. It's also a fun and rewarding experience. I've become much more effective with the feedback I've received, and Scout is a much happier and better-behaved dog.

High-Gain Insights

 The more feedback you receive with an open and objective mind, the more accurate a self-understanding you will have. The more accurate your self-understanding, the more effective you can become.

There are several ways to get feedback. Ideally, over time, you will want to get and give feedback on a regular basis, informally each day and formally at designated times. In order for that to happen, you'll need to create a safe environment around you, develop good listening and feedback skills, and help others to develop theirs.

Here are some Practical Ideas that may help:

A Practice.

- Positive feedback as well as challenging feedback can be awkward to give, so practice as often as possible.

- The goal is to have the words flow clearly and confidently.

- Practice your presentation aloud.

B Get coaching.

- Before you present your performance feedback, practice delivering the feedback to an appropriate individual (skilled, objective, etc.).

- Ask for their feedback on your wording, emphasis, tone, nonverbal cues, etc.

- Make final changes to your communication.

- Practice aloud once again.

C Know your strengths and limits as a feedback-giver.

- If you can't get reasonably comfortable and fluid in your presentation, even with coaching, you may be presenting beyond your limits.

- Get extra coaching to assess what the reasons are:
  - High risk content?
  - Unsure of your content?
  - New at this level of performance feedback?
  - Some "hot button" in you that needs further work?

Performance feedback model:

1. "When you . . . "

    Objectively and specifically describe the work behaviors of the individual.

    _____

    _____

2. " . . . the result(s) was (were) . . . "

    Describe the impact on the organization.

    _____

    _____

    _____

3. Were you aware of the impact?

    _____

    _____

    _____

4. Then, provide an action-based, encouraging go-forward statement.

    Describe goals and the outline of a path forward, e.g., to change negative behavior, reinforce positive behavior, gain new skills, start an initiative, etc.

    _____

    _____

    _____

Examples:

- "When you negotiated unprofitable contract terms with two new major clients, we expanded our gross revenue and client base but lost profitability overall. In fact, the impact was a significant reduction in our yearly bonus to employees."

- "Were you aware of the impact?"

- "The immediate goal for your development is to come to a deeper understanding of contracting and its overall impact on profitability. I suggest you work with me and a task force that will be put together for designing a process that ensures profitability when negotiating major contracts."

Some of the ways to get and give feedback include:

1. Coaching sessions.

2. Mentoring sessions.

3. 360° feedback-assessment instruments.

4. Assessment instruments such as DISC, Myers Briggs, etc.

5. Meeting debriefings.

You earn the right and the credibility to give feedback by asking for, receiving, and constructively responding to feedback. Ask your boss, your peers and your direct reports what they need more of and less of from you. If they hesitate, ask again for just one idea for each question:

More of?

Less of?

Thank them and act upon their best input soon in an observable way. You will increase their trust in, and respect for you.

To quote an ancient Chinese proverb, "The man who removes a mountain begins by carrying away small stones." Learning how to give and get good feedback may not happen overnight. In fact, it may seem daunting, much like moving a mountain. It's alright to take things slowly, one stone at a time. The journey is worthwhile.

"Criticism is necessary and useful; it is often indispensable; but it can never take the place of action, or be even a poor substitute for it."

— THEODORE ROOSEVELT

"There're facts about dogs, and there're opinions about them. The dogs have the facts, and the humans have the opinions."

— THE MONKS OF NEW SKETE, *I & DOG*

CHAPTER 8

Pssssssssst . . . Connect!

One day, I asked my son Matthew how he connected with our dog Scout. He answered, "If you want to connect with Scout, you have to do what *he* wants to do." Good advice from a thirteen-year-old, I thought. In fact, it's what my kids tell me about how to connect with them.

What I love about my relationship with Scout is that we've built such a strong and loving connection without using many words. We read each other through eye contact and body language. Scout knows when I'm happy, when I'm sad, and when it's best to just sit side by side without needing to say or do anything. He knows how to just *be*. That's such a great lesson for someone in my profession who interacts with people all day.

Scout and I also connect by touch. When I pet him, rub his belly, or massage his muscles, Scout experiences my affection for him through my attention and my positive energy. He rolls over on his back, legs up in the air, enjoying the moment of his "doggie massage" and trusting that I won't hurt him in any way. It gives me great joy to make him so happy. Ralph Waldo Emerson once said, "What you do speaks so loud that I cannot hear what you say." I believe that dogs feel the truth of this far more than human beings do.

My friend BJ takes her relationship with dogs to a whole new level. As I mentioned in Chapter 5, BJ havens dogs that have been abandoned and gets them ready for adoption. She takes dogs into her home as part of a foster-care program, and she has three dogs of her own.

BJ Connects at a Deeper Level (In Her Own Words)

 The main part of my connection with my dogs is that they trust me. They know I am safe and gentle, and they respond to me with their own honesty, which means they can make mistakes without fear. My connection comes with the rituals and patterns of their lives. They depend on their daily routine, and my keeping it honors them. Kayla especially is keenly aware of my moods and my actions. If I'm packing for a trip, she sulks on her doggie bed. If I'm crying or angry, she immediately pays attention. If I put on my "doggie coat," she is at the door and ever-hopeful, with a ball in her mouth.

Dogs need to be cautious around people because people have inconsistent responses to dogs, and dogs can get confused so easily. For dogs, life is navigating and living in a land of language that they do not understand. At best, they learn ten to twelve words of our language. The rest is all instinct and learned behavior patterns.

There is a whole-body reaction when dogs connect with other dogs. Tails, eyes, ears, fur, smell, taste, teeth – it's all there and so completely, immediately sense-oriented. In fact, that is their language, all the sensory signs: ears back, fluffed fur, wagging tails. Most dogs are acute interpreters of the instinctive signs of fear and friendship.

Their play is fascinating to watch. My guys wrestle and nuzzle and play-bite with inexhaustible energy. To the untrained eye, it would look hurtful or even angry, but the energy of play is so different from a dogfight, which can be outright vicious.

I cuddle and pet my dogs a lot. We have a morning ritual where I hug and scratch them, and they nuzzle with me. It's all wonderfully in the moment and completely unguarded. Before bed, I'll tell them "goodnight" with more hugs. My dogs actually know what "goodnight" means, and they go to their spots to settle in for the evening. I make eye contact with great gentleness and only rarely for corrections. I find dogs are very sensitive to eye contact. My tone of voice makes more difference than words, and they respond with either surprise or obedience.

What my dogs have taught me about connection is endless and intimate. They have taught me more about my soul, because all of our connections are nonverbal. The brain uses language and the heart uses feelings to communicate, but the soul has its own language and it is not English. So, in a way, my dogs have taught me about what makes my soul sing, or be sad. I have learned a lot more about what nourishes me and what depletes me.

My dogs make me laugh and cry and giggle and feel safe. When Kayla arrived, it was as if a river opened up inside me. Before that, I felt as if I had a clogged artery. I was living an edited life, a compromised existence. Now I could never be without this direct access to my soul. My dogs nourish my soul, and I connect more fearlessly and honestly with the world.

Connect at Work

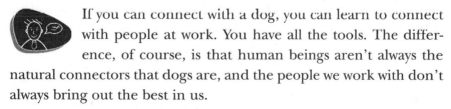 If you can connect with a dog, you can learn to connect with people at work. You have all the tools. The difference, of course, is that human beings aren't always the natural connectors that dogs are, and the people we work with don't always bring out the best in us.

Alfonzo had been telling me for six months how difficult it was to work for his director, Suzanne. Alfonzo was an engineering project manager, and part of a leadership-development program Jim and I ran that involved both group and individual meetings.

The group met in our conference room around a large rectangular table so everyone could see each other easily. Sometimes, during the group meetings, Alfonzo would let the group know about his frustration level with his boss.

"Suzanne just doesn't get it," he'd say. "I can't tell you how close I am to losing it with her."

The group, many of whom knew Suzanne, would listen and express their understanding and support. They would give Alfonzo some strategies to try with Suzanne, and then they'd stay tuned for the next installment.

I scheduled a joint coaching session with me for Alfonzo and Suzanne. Alfonzo would update her on his progress in the program, and they could give each other feedback. I noticed how tense Suzanne appeared as soon as she entered our office. She entered our reception area quietly, timidly, almost like a bird. She refused a cup of coffee and seemed distracted.

Suzanne sat down without a word to anyone, and waited almost motionlessly for Alfonzo to arrive. She didn't notice me watching her from my office. It struck me how completely out of place she looked, as if she'd wandered into a minefield and was waiting to be rescued.

Alfonzo, who had been nothing less than warm and friendly during all of our sessions, arrived five minutes later. He became polite but standoffish as soon as he saw Suzanne. He sat down in a chair that couldn't have been farther away from Suzanne. I could tell this session was going to be a challenge.

I came out and ushered them into a private room. I offered a warm and inviting "hello" to reassure both of them that they were welcome and could relax, but neither of them softened.

I introduced an agenda that I hoped would provide some structure to our conversation.

Alfonzo sat on the edge of his chair and said, "I've learned a lot through this program, Suzanne. I've gotten a bit more assertive.

I don't hate conflict as much as I did before, and I'm learning that not everything is my responsibility. So I guess I'm delegating more, which was one of your concerns. I'm not just an engineering geek who hides himself in his office anymore. I'm actually listening to the people on my team, not just to my bosses, and I think it's paying off."

"Tell us about how you've worked on becoming more assertive," I said.

He thought about this for a moment.

"I'm not procrastinating as much. When I don't know how to do something or whom to ask, I'm finding out sooner. I'm not paralyzed in unfamiliar situations."

I noticed how Suzanne took detailed notes while Alfonzo spoke, not lifting her eyes from the page, but following along carefully with her pen.

When Alfonzo was finished, Suzanne, in a very soft voice, said, "I've noticed more people at your door, Alfonzo. People are coming by to have you solve problems, and you're much more approachable. You're also keeping all the balls in the air, which is good. You aren't getting as frustrated as you used to. And most of all, you're not getting as rattled by interruptions. You really seem to be rolling with things a lot better."

Alfonzo smiled weakly, trying to look pleased that his boss had complimented him, but it didn't look to me as if he really felt that way. Now it was his turn to give Suzanne some feedback.

"You're not spending time developing us," he said.

"If you speak about yourself instead of 'us,' " I told him, "Suzanne will understand you better, and your feedback will be more powerful."

Alfonzo nodded.

"OK, OK. Suzanne, you're not spending time developing *me*. When we get together for our one-on-ones, we only talk about business issues. I feel like you're using me as an information tool, not valuing me as a person. You're not encouraging."

He shifted uncomfortably in his chair.

"You always make it seem like you have more important things to do than meet with me. So I end up letting you off the hook. We don't meet very often, and I wind up feeling . . . I don't know . . . bad . . ."

Suzanne didn't react at all. Even her pen had stopped moving.

"Also," Alfonzo continued, "you're not connecting enough with the people who've been at the company for a long time. When you do come out of your office, you tend to ask the new people how they're doing – which is fine, there's nothing wrong with that – but then you completely ignore the veterans."

I glanced over at Suzanne and saw that she had begun to cry. Her tears flowed quietly, almost unnoticeably at first. Her expression remained unchanged. I was stunned into silence. I think Alfonzo was, too. His mouth hung slightly open and he leaned away from her.

"Thank you for telling me these things, Alfonzo," she managed with a surprisingly steady voice. "I know I haven't been doing very well, but it's good to get that out in the open. I feel like I haven't been able to be myself for the last few years. There's been too much work and too little time. I'm working twelve hours a day and my boss keeps piling on more."

I offered Suzanne a tissue. She took it gratefully and continued.

"I'm a much more outgoing person outside of work. I used to be one inside of work, too. I just feel too much pressure now. The pressure . . . "

"I know," said Alfonzo. "We all feel it. You're not alone. It's difficult."

"You're right," Suzanne said, "and I want to do better." The tears had finally stopped, and Suzanne seemed less tense. She was beginning to open up to Alfonzo in a way he wasn't expecting. He continued to be a bit guarded, but he watched Suzanne with a less combative eye.

I walked to the large easel pad that is always set up in my office. I drew two concentric circles with a thick red marker. I put Suzanne's name in the center of the bull's-eye.

"You're the boss and you need to have healthy connections with everyone on your team. When people are inside the bull's-eye with you, they're too close. When they're outside the second circle, they're too far away. Each person on the team needs to be between the first and the second circles, with equal connection and access to you and with each other. Does that make sense?"

Suzanne and Alfonzo both agreed.

"Where do you feel you are on the circles, Alfonzo?" Suzanne asked.

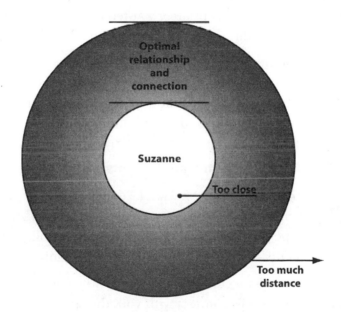

"I feel outside of the second circle," he replied.

Suzanne nodded.

"I sometimes feel outside of your circle, too. You and Steve get together a lot in the department and commiserate about me, or at least that's what I think. I feel ganged-up on by the two of you."

There was a pause. Silence can be a great facilitator. I let it stand until Suzanne asked me, "So where do we go from here?"

"You start by building healthy connections," I said. "Just like you're doing today. By being real with each other, by talking about your relationship, by letting your guard down a bit and saying what it feels like to be you, in your world."

I glanced at my watch and realized that an hour and a half had gone by in an instant, and we needed to close the meeting. I gave both of them affirming feedback for such fine work, and then I did something I rarely feel comfortable doing. I approached Alfonzo and gave him a hug. I went to Suzanne and hugged her, too. Never mind that hugging just "wasn't done" in corporate America, at that moment, I knew it was appropriate. I wanted them to feel how proud I was of them for the difficult work they'd done.

The best moment of all came when I watched Suzanne and Alfonzo hug each other, too. I could see that it was the beginning of a completely new level of connection between them, and they now had a fighting chance to make their situation better.

High-Gain Insights

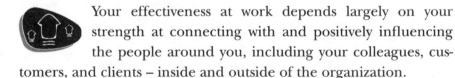 Your effectiveness at work depends largely on your strength at connecting with and positively influencing the people around you, including your colleagues, customers, and clients – inside and outside of the organization.

The more you connect with people in healthy ways and the more access you give others to connect with you, the stronger your ability to influence your organization and the better your life becomes.

Motivational speaker Anthony Robbins once said, "The way we communicate with others and with ourselves ultimately determines the quality of our lives." I don't think that's an exaggeration.

It may be that not all of your relationships are as effective as they could be.

Following are some Practical Ideas that may help you strengthen your connections.

Using the emotional-connection chart that follows, plot all of the key relationships around you, including your boss, peers, people who report directly to you, and those who simply may be in your sphere of influence.

- Which people are in the center ring with you? They are too close, and that makes it difficult for you to be objective about them. It also makes it difficult for others to break in.

- Which people are outside of the blue area? They are too distant, and that makes it difficult for them to feel as if you are accessible to them.

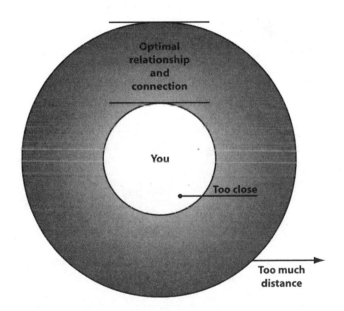

Factors affecting emotional connection:
- Rapport (natural)
- Competence
- Role interdependence

- Try to figure out how to put all of your key relationships in the blue area, each equally connecting with you and with each other. That's the place of healthy connection and the proper distance for being objective.

Optimal professional relationships, emotional connection, and high performance:

"Dealing with people is probably the biggest problem you face, especially if you are in business. Yes, and that is also true if you are a housewife, architect, or engineer."

— DALE CARNEGIE

"What dogs want most in life is for no one to go away."

— JOSE SARAMAGO

CHAPTER 9

If You Want to Have Fewer Conflicts, Have More of Them[1]

Frankly, I don't know many people who love conflict. Clients don't typically come to my office rubbing their hands together and itching to have a good fight at work. They're more likely to want to avoid or delay disagreement, hoping it will magically disappear, than they are to want to address the issue with the other person directly.

Conflicts are challenging whether they're with peers or whether they involve someone in a different power position. When you have equal power, you both rely on your influence. When you have the power, the other person may feel more at risk, but not always. When you don't have the power, you're likely to feel more challenged to resolve the issue.

---

[1] This is a paraphrase of quotes from Ron Kraybill: "If you want to have less conflict, try to have more." If people scratch their heads at this, he would clarify: "A more precise way to put this might be, 'If you want less conflict, invite disagreement.' " Ron Kraybill is a professor in the Conflict Transformation Program at Eastern Mennonite University and founder of Riverhouse ePress, a Web and print publisher of resources on conflict transformation, at *www.RiverhouseEpress.com.*

If you're going to work on your conflict-management skills, here's a working definition I've always found true:

Conflict is an emotionally charged struggle that arises from differences in values, needs, or competing claims to resources, such as time, money, space, or position.

Understanding the nature of conflict puts you in a better position to resolve the conflict. Being able to have healthy conflicts is critical to your long-term effectiveness at work. Healthy conflicts are useful when you're trying to push the envelope on new ideas and want to innovate. When people know that conflict is a positive experience, and that you don't lose your cool or hold onto resentments, they will feel safe to disagree with you.

If people feel safe to disagree with you, they'll let you know about issues early. They'll give you the opportunity to address them before they loom larger. When people know you're open to new ideas that are different from your own, they'll also let you know about ways to make improvements without having to worry about your reaction. Potential conflicts are easier to resolve the more openly you address them. That's why we say, if you want to have fewer conflicts, *have more of them.*

A conflict has usually gone on for some time before I become involved. Something is at stake, and emotions are running high.

Ben came to my office with a pensive look on his face. He was deep in thought and looked vaguely troubled. I tried to read his expression for a while.

Finally, I asked, "How are you? You look like you're thinking about something. Care to share it with me?"

"Yeah, sure," he said. "There's a problem I need to talk through about one of my key people. I'm in the midst of a difficult situation, and I need some help in handling it."

"Alright, let's get to it."

"I have a manager who works for me. Her name is Michelle. She knows her stuff and handles a lot of clients' work really well. I depend on Michelle for a whole lot of things. The department would only run about half as well without her."

Ben's gaze shifted downward. He was staring at the table as he talked. I cocked my head to see if I could encourage him to make eye contact, but he wasn't interested.

"Michelle and I used to be close, but in the last year we haven't been getting along. We've drifted apart. About a year ago, I gave her a low raise. She didn't like it and told me so. Things haven't been the same since then. I'm worried."

Curious about what happened, I asked, "Why did you give her a low raise?"

Now he looked up.

"She made a couple of mistakes on clients' work. She hadn't staffed her department well enough. A couple of positions were open too long. And some of the department managers were complaining that she was negative to work with."

"What's her behavior been like over the last year? Be as specific as you can."

"She's unhappy, negative, moody, tired. She complains a lot, calls in sick, and she has a habit of being sarcastic. If I'm going to be completely honest, I also think she's bad-mouthing me behind my back, and that's really pissing me off."

"It sounds like you're both pretty angry with each other. And this has been going on for a year? What took you so long to address it?"

"I hate stuff like this. I had hoped this one would blow over, but it hasn't. It was a mistake not to address it. Now it's serious."

"How serious?"

"Not sure. Can you work with Michelle and help her figure it out?" he asked.

"I can work with both of you, but there's no guarantee on the out-come. Michelle has to *want* to work this out. And you have to want to hear the issues and work them out, too. That means getting past the anger and resentment, and really listening. Are you ready to do that?"

"It's better than the alternative."

From the first time I met with Michelle, I was concerned about how this was going to go. Michelle rarely made eye contact with me. She shifted frequently in her chair, looking out the windows, studying the glass partitions that separated us from the waiting area. Whenever she heard a telephone ring or someone outside my office, she became distracted. I often repeated questions to her and asked her for more direct answers, which she found hard to give.

She wasn't really sure why she had to meet with me. She thought things between her and Ben had gotten better and she didn't under-stand why talking about this was necessary.

It took several meetings for Michelle to open up and trust that it was safe to talk to me in confidence. She acknowledged that she had been angry with Ben in the past, but she insisted she was over it. She had gotten a better raise recently and that helped smooth things over.

Michelle said it was hard to talk about issues with Ben because she was afraid she could lose her job, which she liked, if she wasn't careful. I explained that without talking about the issues in a safe environment, they might *never* get resolved to either of their satisfac-tions. I also explained that Ben had issues he wanted to talk about with Michelle, and I wanted to help her get ready to hear them.

So I worked with each of them separately. I helped Michelle prepare to talk about her problems with Ben. And I helped Ben prepare several concerns he wanted to talk about with Michelle. I still wondered how things would go when the three of us met. I reminded myself of David Hume's wise words: "Truth springs from argument amongst friends." I knew that if I could break through their defenses and remind them of their friendship, success would follow. I made it my responsibility to make sure they saw that.

Unfortunately, on the day of their meeting, neither one of their hearts seemed to be in it. Although they had each done some good preparation, something was holding them back. Michelle seemed not to trust that she could be honest with Ben without fear of consequences. And Ben, while he had developed some insight about himself, didn't want to push Michelle past her comfort zone.

We met together once more. Words were spoken, but the desire to make things better was missing. Neither one reached out or tried hard to connect. In fact, I was trying harder than both of them together. I tried to get them talking about their mutual successes and some of the struggles they'd been through together. I tried to get them to discuss their future hopes and aspirations. I tried to get them to identify their problems.

Neither of them opened up. Neither of them asked questions of each other. And neither of them wanted to come back for another session. I think the risk was too high for Ben and Michelle, and the benefits, too uncertain.

I recently learned that they were still working together, but I often wonder how happy they are, or if they're happy at all.

*　　*　　*

German author Hans Magnus Enzensberger once wrote, "Animals fight, but they do not wage war." Dogs can get aggressive when they are threatened and become protective when they are afraid. Their conflicts tend to be situational and short, and they don't hold on to resentment. Those are all great traits. Do you think we humans could learn something from them? I sure do. Let me give you a quick example that Bob, our dog trainer, described to me.

He had a client with an eighty-pound, eight-year-old Otter Hound. If a neighbor came by, the dog lunged at the neighbor. He was aggressive toward strangers as well. The dog's owner tried petting and talking to the dog to calm him, but nothing worked.

Bob decided to teach the owner a somewhat-complicated maneuver called "behavioral interrupts." He showed the owner how to frame her eyes, physically, with her hands, and command the dog to "Watch me!" when people came around. In increasing levels of stress, the framing and "Watch me!" command refocused the dog on his owner, rather than the visitor. This, followed with positive verbal reinforcement, "Good boy!" and the all-important treat, began to fix the problem. It took awhile, but now the Otter Hound behaves as if he knows good things happen for him when he's around other people.

*　　*　　*

For many humans, behavioral changes can be quite a challenge, too. The situation I was asked to moderate between Priscilla and Emily is a perfect example.

Priscilla had come to a conclusion: Her relationship with Emily, one of her peers at work, had to get better because it couldn't get worse. Every time these two were in a meeting together, they butted heads. Priscilla would say "up," and Emily would say "down." Priscilla would say "yes," and Emily would say "no." There seemed to be no subjects upon which they could agree, and no one was enjoying their debates, least of all, their boss.

Priscilla decided she was going to have to face Emily in a non-threatening way. Neither of them held the power of a higher position. This would be a good test of Priscilla's conflict-resolution skills, something we had covered in our group sessions. She was motivated to make this relationship better for her own sake.

Emily was new to the team. She was a nice person, according to Priscilla. But she had strong opinions on a lot of things and she wasn't shy about offering them. She had come from a competitor and was hired to broaden this team's perspective. She stuck to her own job and rarely volunteered to help on team projects. Priscilla surmised that Emily was trying to make her mark, but it sure didn't feel good to Priscilla when it came at her expense.

Priscilla and I worked on becoming clear about what she felt the issues were and if Emily would be receptive to these. We also came up with some feedback she would give to her. Since the situation had been going on for only about a month, it hadn't escalated too far.

Priscilla decided that she needed to understand Emily's opinions better, determine what was important to her, and figure out how she was feeling as the newest member of the team, which couldn't be easy.

Priscilla also decided to tell her that it upset her when Emily took contrary views in meetings. It didn't bother Priscilla that she and Emily disagreed; it was how Emily did it and how many times it happened.

Emily would say things like, "Here's how we did it at my former company, and it worked really well." This made Priscilla feel devalued, as if her opinions didn't matter.

She jotted down several other pieces of feedback, practiced them, and was ready to give it a try with Emily.

When we reconvened a few weeks later, Priscilla reported that she and Emily had made some good initial strides. Emily had listened and apologized for offending Priscilla in the meetings. She also told Priscilla that they genuinely disagreed on a number of topics and that she didn't think Priscilla was very open to new ideas.

Priscilla thought she would need to work on that one. Emily had brought a new level of experience to the team, and she was a strong personality. The truth was, Emily intimidated her a bit. Priscilla needed to look at the possibility that maybe she was being a bit defensive.

Priscilla had done the right thing, and it sounded as if she had done it well. She had addressed the conflict with Emily early, before it had a chance to escalate. She had given Emily feedback in a respectful way, and Emily had respected Priscilla's points of view.

Priscilla and Emily would still need to continue talking things through. I suggested they take on a project together. I was confident that with continued attention, their relationship would grow in a positive direction.

High-Gain Insights

We often find that people who avoid conflicts have a lot of unresolved conflicts around them. Conflict-management skills are learnable and they are skills that will benefit you in work and in life. It's always good to keep in mind that conflict is an essential part of growth. General George S. Patton once said, "If everyone is thinking alike, then somebody isn't thinking." If we all foster that kind of an open mind when it comes to conflict, imagine how much we can learn and improve.

Some people are better at managing conflicts than others. They've probably worked hard at developing their skills. You can, too. The following are some Practical Ideas that will help you manage conflict in healthy ways:

1. Know and manage yourself.

   • Understand your current feelings (see list in Chapter 6), emotional hot buttons, and triggers. Remember not to confront when you're angry.

2. Deal directly with the person with whom you have the conflict.

   • Know who the stakeholder(s) are in the conflict.

   • The only way to resolve the conflict is by working directly with the person or people involved.

3. Prepare for the conflict.

   • Think about what's really important to you and what's important to the other party (values, principles, pride, etc.).

   • Identify your needs and current positions, but don't be rigid.

   • Imagine the other party's positions on the issues. What are their hot buttons?

   • Get coaching and guidance from an objective third party.

- Practice.
- Expect the unexpected.

4. Have the conflict discussion.

   - Listen closely.
   - Speak succinctly; less is more in trying to get your points across.
   - Keep checking in with the other party or parties to make sure they are feeling understood.
   - Read and respond to emotions in yourself and others along the way.
   - Take it as far as you both can, productively.
   - Schedule another time to continue if necessary.

5. Don't create unhealthy triangles.

   - Talking with other people about the conflict, other than to get coaching and guidance about how to deal with the issues, can escalate the conflict as people take sides.

6. Consider having an objective third party in the room.

   - If there's a lot at stake and emotions are running high, it may be best to have someone who can help facilitate the discussion.

Remember to utilize this process as early in a conflict situation as possible before it grows more intense and more complicated.

"Whenever you're in conflict with someone, there is one factor that can make the difference between damaging your relationship and deepening it. That factor is attitude."

– WILLIAM JAMES

CHAPTER 10
Enhance Your Clarity

Years ago I met a man who impressed me so much with his clarity, I'll never forget him. His name was Jim, and he ran a prison ministry program. Jim visited prisons every week and conducted emotional-processing groups for inmates who had committed serious crimes. Most of these folks weren't getting out of prison soon, and many of them were lifers.

In addition, he ran a ministry-funded restaurant in the city that employed ex-cons who were re-entering society. The restaurant provided them with stable employment, a fair wage, and taught them the discipline and habits they would need to function out in the world.

When I met Jim he was in his thirties. He took me and several others into the prison for one of his weekly group sessions. Like everyone else, I was there to listen, learn, and participate.

I had rarely heard someone speak as clearly as Jim and I nick-named him "Clear as a Bell Jim." Jim knew who he was and why he was committed to this prison ministry work. He didn't do it for the money, and it was obvious that he loved his work.

When he spoke, every word counted. He didn't add anything extraneous, didn't cut short his thoughts, and he was straightforward and honest. His emotions were congruent with his speech. You always knew where Jim stood; he had no hidden agendas.

It was clear that the inmates connected to Jim. Lifers in prison who have committed every crime imaginable – and some you *can't* imagine – have seen it all. You can't bullshit them; they can spot a phony from miles away. You have to know who you are, what you believe in, your biases, and your prejudices, and you have to be willing to talk straight to them. Lifers have nothing to lose, and they don't suffer fools.

Jim was the kind of person who put it out there and didn't apologize. He also didn't judge or lecture. I only went to the prison with Jim once, but I'll never forget him and my experience there. I truly admire Jim's clarity. I hope, on a good day, I can be half as clear and steady as Jim, especially in the face of tough situations.

Diamond on the Green

 Our son Matthew's baseball season started recently, and we were on the field on a Saturday night for the first game. Baseball season is a wonderful time for the kids and their families. For the kids, it's prime time for their growing athleticism, teamwork, skills, and confidence. For the parents, we're full of pride, encouragement, camaraderie, and, let's face it, the opportunity to just sit down in a chair for a few hours without doing the ten other things we should be doing.

We line the field with our multicolored folding chairs, each family sitting on their son's side of the field. My chair is blue. It's the cool one with the built-in footrest upon which the other parents always comment. My husband Terry, being the kind man he is, yearns in silence for the chair with the footrest. In the upstate New York spring weather, we have to dress warmly. Even on warm days, by the time early evening arrives, we wrap ourselves with multiple layers of blankets, hats, hoods, and even gloves for those night games.

For me, baseball season also holds a wonderful secret; it's a chance for me to meet some new dogs and see how the dogs from last season have grown.

I first glimpsed my new canine interest out of the corner of my right eye as she came tearing onto the field. I turned just in time to catch a bouncing blur of black-and-white fur with a long lead flapping behind her. She bounded happily up to her family members, craving their attention. Going from person to person, she jumped, twirled, licked, and then raced over to the grass where she buried herself into the electric green grass, rolling and twisting until the smell of that beautiful earth coated her like a new perfume.

Along with the dog came the girl with the beautiful long, light-brown hair. She had fair skin, wore glasses, and had a gentle smile. I knew by the way she carried herself that she was an old soul in a young girl's body. She wrapped and tied the dog's long pink lead around her waist, connecting herself at one end and the dog at the other like a bow on a present. It was clear she was going to be in charge.

During the entire game, the dog literally chomped at her bit, whimpered as she saw dogs wandering on the outskirts of the field, and tried to dodge onto the field at various times. The girl with the beautiful long hair walked her far away from the field at one point. Each time I watched her, I noticed that she was calm, centered, and serious with the dog, exerting her authority and at the same time, giving her dog lots of love.

I walked over to meet the girl and the dog about midway through the game.

"What's her name," I asked.

"Diamond," she answered.

"What's your name?"

"Jenna," she replied.

Diamond could barely contain herself. She began to bounce and jump toward me while the girl did all she could to restrain her.

I said, "Your dog is adorable. What kind of dog is she?"

After telling me she was part Cavalier King Charles Spaniel and part Border Collie, she announced, "She's as bad as she is cute. She's six months old. She's eaten everything we have at home. Look, she's even chewed her lead. But, I love her."

"I can tell," I said. "You handle her well."

"I'm obsessed with dogs," she replied clearly. "I have a dog business, too. I walk dogs and take care of them when their owners are away. I do whatever people want."

I smiled. What a delightful girl. Focused. Centered. Clear. And all from a girl of about ten-years old. I certainly didn't have that kind of presence at her age, and I still strive for such clarity today.

She's a future leader, I thought.

I walked back to my folding chair on that cool spring night in May and gazed at the setting sun. I realized that while I was initially drawn to Diamond, it was Jenna, the girl with the beautiful long hair, who was clearly the true gem. I'm looking forward to more time getting to know Jenna during baseball season, and watching Diamond grow up, too.

Clear About Some Things . . . and Not About Others

 I agreed to work with someone who was starting up a consulting business. Carol was an unusual client for our firm because when she came to us, she didn't have any staff. She was early in her business-development curve. Typically, business people go several years before wanting to work on their development, which is an unfortunate commentary on priorities in our current business culture.

But Carol was not typical. She was clear about needing and wanting help, and that was the first thing that impressed me about her. She had an unwavering commitment to her business and a strong work ethic. She would work around the clock if she needed to meet deadlines to satisfy her clients. I could see she was very talented, yet she struggled to forge her way in a highly competitive industry. But I could see three things very clearly: she had the talent to succeed, she had the drive to succeed, and she was relentless.

That said, Carol was not as clear about how to manage the emotional ups and downs inherent in her chosen path. She was the primary wage earner in her family and had two children to support. Self-employment is a risky path for anyone. Although we were both convinced she could make this work, she was often fearful and anxious during deals that took time to put together and time to come to fruition. She had a hard time staying steady in the face of risk and uncertainty. This was understandable. The stakes were pretty high, and the risks were all her own.

But she was beginning to show signs of strain. She noticed that she was becoming curt with her children. She was getting testy with clients. And I noticed that she often seemed restless and impatient with me.

At one of our sessions, I decided to go deeper with Carol. I was convinced that if she could understand how she came across to people, she could make some adjustments and increase her effectiveness. I knew she had everything it took to run a consulting business, and the successes were starting to build. But she was on the verge of landing her biggest deal, and it was obvious to me that this was playing havoc with her nerves.

We sat across from each other in my office with Carol's papers spread across my round mahogany table. She was always so intent on working through business issues that I had to pull her focus away to change the subject. I leaned in and looked her straight in the eyes.

"Carol, you have everything you need to be successful in your business, and the results are starting to come in. But I'm concerned about you and the way you come across sometimes. I'm worried about how that could play with your clients."

"What do you mean?" she asked.

I didn't want Carol to think I was challenging her. I sat back and tried to sound neutral.

"Sometimes you seem angry and edgy, maybe even a little impatient and abrupt. I can handle it just fine because I know you and trust you, but I wonder if you do that with clients."

"I'm intense," she said, "especially when I'm nervous. But, jeez, that's not a problem, is it? Don't you think clients like intensity?"

"What happens to your clarity when you get so intense?" I asked.

"Well . . . I suppose sometimes I lose a little control," Carol admitted, "and then I'm vulnerable to snap decisions, which might not be so good."

"That's true for all of us," I added. "But you have a lot at stake here. I'm recommending you get some insight into what's happening so you can manage yourself better and maintain your clarity."

"OK," she said, a little reluctantly. She moved aside her papers and gave me her full attention.

"What's underneath that sudden anger that I sometimes see?"

Carol had to think about that for a while.

"Fear of not being enough," she answered. "Wondering whether I can really do this. Wondering what I'll do if I fail."

"What do you do when you get angry and fearful?"

"I disconnect, I guess, withdraw from the situation and the people involved. I push them away before they can reject me."

"Think about that," I said. "Can you see what would happen to your business if you did that all the time, if it became habitual?"

"Yes. And I can't afford to let that happen. But my fear is real."

"I know it's real, and some of that intensity might put the business at risk right when you need a clear head."

"What do I do?" she asked. "I'm about to embark on the most important business trip of my career, and I don't want to blow it."

"Let's become clear about what you want to accomplish when you go. Let's discuss the people with whom you'll be meeting and identify what's important to them. Then, let's determine how you can connect with them positively and productively."

Carol visibly relaxed and quickly refocused. It took only a few minutes for a clear plan to emerge once she was unencumbered by her fear.

She closed the session by saying, "I had no idea we were going to wind up here. Wow, I have a headache. I never thought I'd say this to anyone, but thanks for the headache. I really needed it."

Carol went off on her business trip the following week. Things went well and everything looked promising, but she hadn't quite been able to close the deal. Her prospective client wanted to think things over and consider some other options.

The next few weeks were torture for Carol. We traded e-mails several times. She tried to stay calm. She stayed connected with her prospective client. And then it happened: she got the call to finalize the biggest contract of her career.

Carol was ecstatic for all of sixty seconds. Then she immediately turned her attention to figuring out how she was going to get the work done that they wanted in such a short period of time.

I'm not worried. I know Carol will do an amazing job for this client, and that her business will take off. After all, she has the talent and the drive to succeed, and she's relentless. About this, we're both clear.

High-Gain Insights

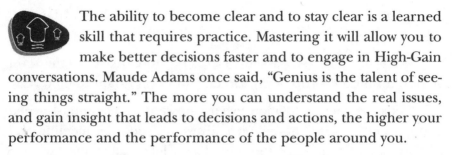 The ability to become clear and to stay clear is a learned skill that requires practice. Mastering it will allow you to make better decisions faster and to engage in High-Gain conversations. Maude Adams once said, "Genius is the talent of seeing things straight." The more you can understand the real issues, and gain insight that leads to decisions and actions, the higher your performance and the performance of the people around you.

The following is our "Clarity in Action^{SM}" model that we have developed for enhancing clarity and for "making better decisions faster." It starts in the upper-right-hand segment with having the "courage to know and be yourself." Remember these two principles as you move through the process:

1. All aspects of clarity are rooted in the spirit of curiosity and inquiry.

2. High-Gain questioning is the force that helps drive you toward more clarity.

Clarity in Action model steps:

- Have the courage to know and be yourself. You are the leverage point for important decisions and action. You must know and understand yourself.

- Question reality. Develop a true commitment to seeing reality and seeking answers that provide insight to effective action. Stay open no matter where the truth leads.

- Identify the right issue. Use the "right questions" to determine the most important issue for your focus and decision-making.

- Engage in High-Gain conversations. Dialogue with key people and in ways that lead to valuable High-Gain conversations and move you toward the results you desire.

- Gain insight. Upon reflection, what do you see and feel? What deeper understanding, awareness, or "Aha!" has the process provided? Take time to reflect upon possible actions and outcomes.

- Decide. This is the decision point. To what are you willing to commit? Determine your plan of action.

- Act. Move forward to take the steps and complete the tasks necessary to implement your decision. You achieve the results.

- Review and respond. Assess how well your decisions and actions have helped you succeed. Make any changes or alterations to your action. Once again, act with renewed focus and clarity.

"More important than the quest for certainty is the quest for clarity."
– FRANCOIS GAUTIER

CHAPTER 11
Focus and Finish

If you've ever seen a dog stalking prey or have approached a dog with a bone, you know how tenacious and determined they can be. Dogs have an uncanny ability to focus on a single activity when it's something they really want. Undistracted and undeterred, they go after what they want and see it through to the end.

When my dog Scout receives a bone, it's the highlight of his day. Protective of it, he takes the bone into his crate, chewing, gnawing, and slobbering. It's real down-and-dirty dog stuff. He'll work at it until every last bit of meat is gone. Then he'll crack the bone into bits and grind it down until virtually nothing is left.

Scout can be just as relentless when he sees a person or dog through the glass panel of our front door. He'll bark and scratch and make laser eye contact. He'll claw at the window, hoping I'll open the front door so he can get a better look. It's as if nothing else in the world matters at that moment.

I watched a television program one evening where a spry young dog, a Boxer, had mastered opening coconuts on one of the Hawaiian Islands. His owners knocked the coconuts down from the trees and left them in a box outdoors. The Boxer then began the long process of breaking into them by removing their hairy and rugged exteriors. This was not an easy task. He pulled each section off with his teeth until he was left with the hard shell.

Then, with the hard shell exposed, the Boxer struggled to get the coconut positioned just right in his jaws so he could crack it open. Finally, after hours of work, the coconut cracked, rewarding him with milk and meat as a delightful treat for his efforts. The owners said this task now occupied most of the dog's time.

The incredible determination of dogs is an inspiring lesson for everyone, especially when you think about how you can benefit from improving your ability to focus and finish things better at work.

Focus at Work

 Finding and maintaining your focus at work can be a challenge. You have deadlines to meet. Customers want it *now*. Your boss wants it yesterday. Everything can seem like a top priority.

One of my clients has a daily numbering system where she lists her top three priorities of the day to remind her to increase productivity. She has to constantly prompt herself at every meeting and in every e-mail that it's *productivity* that counts.

Another client is constantly changing priorities. He's an "idea guy." He comes in on a Monday morning and has ten new ideas before nine o'clock. In meetings he is constantly generating new thoughts. Sometimes that's great, but as good as the ideas are, they don't always seem to come to fruition. The commitment and follow-through aren't there, and the people around him get frustrated.

One manager with whom I worked has three unchanging priorities for his business: Get it done right the first time. Get it out to the customer within seven days. If you can't get it out to the customer within seven days, call him and let him know when he can expect it.

Susan Scott, in her book *Fierce Conversations*, talks about the difference between digging one hundred wells, each a foot deep and three wells one hundred-feet deep. You're more likely to strike oil in the three wells. Focusing can make you more productive.

Kenny's Story

 For some real insight into focus, what it means, and how important an attribute it is, you must read Kenny's incredible story. He's one of the most focused and special people I know. From the time he was a little boy, he wanted to be an engineer, just like his dad. While other kids were out playing sports, Kenny was inside tinkering with gadgets. He was fascinated with how things worked. He took apart toasters, phones, cameras, and just about anything he could get his hands on that had moving parts.

Soon Kenny began assembling and inventing things. One summer evening, while visiting us, he fashioned a hot-air balloon from a dry-cleaning bag, aluminum foil, and a can of Sterno fuel. The balloon soared, dancing through the sky at dusk, delighting the kids and adults in the neighborhood.

Kenny's story is truly remarkable, but no one can tell it better than he can.

Kenny's Got a Focus and a Dream (In His Own Words)

 So there I was, sitting in the one place that I least wanted to be: freshman high-school algebra class. It was a brilliantly sunny day and my thoughts soon drifted to one of my obsessions: the solar-powered death ray! Oh, to dream. I had this surreal vision of myself cooking a hot dog with a beam of light bridging across space and time. So then I tried to imagine how that would be done, and that was the genesis of the Collapsible, Portable

Parabolic Solar Grill. Just then the teacher called on me, and I had absolutely no idea what was going on in class.

I was in the school system's LD program. LD means "learning-disabled." It's true; I freely admit it. I had some pretty severe learning disabilities, some of them you may have heard of, some of them you probably haven't. I was the slowest kid in the slowest class, and some of these kids didn't even graduate from high school. My mental math skills were so bad, I couldn't even play cards. To be in the LD program, you had to be evaluated every three years by a neuropsychologist. They wanted to make sure you actually had a learning disability in order to justify all that money the government was throwing at you to make sure you weren't "left behind," and to see if you were making any progress.

Well, every three years I would take their IQ and achievement tests and thoroughly enjoyed watching these people stare at the results in disbelief. I would totally max out the test at both ends – measure in at an extremely low percentage for math and spelling, while scoring above the ninety-fifth percentile in other areas. I was reading at a college level in elementary school and had science and spatial-reasoning skills to match, but I couldn't spell better than someone in kindergarten. All the while I was making inventions and winning national science competitions. I was even written up in my local newspaper for my numerous inventions, all before high school.

I have Attention Deficit Disorder (ADD). Not the "Oh-I-can't-concentrate-I-must-have-ADD" kind, but the clinically diagnosed, seriously debilitating variety. ADD is a fascinating beast: hyperactivity and lack of focus, punctuated by hyper-focus. Just watch a kid with ADD play video games for twelve hours straight and you'll begin to get the idea.

But I'm not the type of person to let ADD or anything else stop me. I wanted the Collapsible, Portable Parabolic Solar Grill to become a reality, so I had to convert the two-dimensional drawings I'd made into a three-dimensional design that required 150 individual articulating mirrors to form a parabolic reflector in three-dimensional space and then fold down to 2D again. The whole deal ended up looking like some sort of B-movie sci-fi device, a bazaar series of aluminum fins to soak up every little ray of sunlight and convert it to hot-dog-cooking thermal power.

The invention was a total success. I started bringing it to school and grilling hot dogs in the noontime sun. My classmates thought it was cool, but they still thought I was a total nerd. I took the grill to the beach many times, watched it work perfectly, and always attracted a big crowd of people who wanted to know where they could buy one. But math continued to be a horrible problem for me. I never got any better, no matter how hard I tried, no matter how hard I focused. Why was I still the worst math student in every class I took?

In my senior year of high school, something extraordinary happened to me. I had attracted the attention of a top neuroscience researcher from the National Institutes of Health (NIH). He became very interested in my case. He told me that he was working on a research study that involved trying to understand why some stroke victims completely lost their math ability and what it could tell us about the brain. I agreed to work with him and his team.

The researchers needed to look directly into my head to see exactly what was going on. The answer came in the form of a technology that was brand-new at the time: Functional MRI Spectroscopy. This machine did what was formerly impossible, not just track blood flow, but track specific neurotransmitters and see where they went during certain thought processes.

As it turned out, I had what the doctors described as "an area of dysfunction" in the brain. There is a very special spot designated to do math, and although it structurally existed for me, the neurotransmitters just weren't firing. I also had atypical chemical distributions in my brain, which basically meant that I was literally thinking differently from other human beings. I was told if I would have suffered the same damage as an adult, I would have been incapacitated. Other stroke victims couldn't even participate in the study because they couldn't have performed the tests.

So I completely took advantage of the latest technology to help me out. My spelling problem was solved with voice-recognition software almost immediately, and if I'd only had computer-aided design (CAD) in high school, I could have solved the parabola problem instantaneously. Of course the problem with math was a big one. I struggled through every math class and failed calculus four times!

As I write this, I've been in college for six years. I haven't stopped inventing things. I even managed to land an internship as a technical engineer. College has been the greatest challenge of my life. While other students were enjoying their weekends and their spring breaks, all I cared about was pulling my course "incompletes" and failures up to at least passing grades. I got a lot of tutoring help from the services offered by my college, but nothing compared to the help and support I received from my professors who believed in me. Without them, I never would have survived. I don't even know at this point if I will actually graduate. There is still no guarantee. There really are no guarantees in life, if you want to know the truth. But I'm not going to quit. You can count on that.

Not too long after Kenny wrote this, he was at a party hosted by the dean of the college. Unbeknownst to Kenny, the CEO whose engineering company he'd been interning with was there. The CEO had met and talked to Kenny during his internship, and he had admired Kenny's drive and passion for inventing, and his talent and ingenuity. He had decided that he'd like to see Kenny working for him full time, but he wanted to surprise Kenny and make the offer in person. The dean's party would be the perfect opportunity. Kenny had no idea what was in store for him.

When the CEO arrived at the party, he walked straight across the room, smiling ear to ear. He shook Kenny's hand and said, "I wanted to see you in person. As soon as you graduate, I'd like to have you on board at my company full time as an engineer. What do you say?"

As Kenny described the moment, he had no idea what to say. He stood speechless for what seemed an eternity, until he felt tears beginning to well in his eyes. After all of his struggles, his dream was going to come true, and he would be working as an engineer at last.

"I'll take that as a yes," the CEO finally said, saving Kenny from having to speak.

I don't mind telling you that this is one of my favorite stories. I've heard many very successful people say that we should never work to acquire, but to *become*, because it's the becoming that brings us joy, not the acquiring. I couldn't be happier for Kenny, a young man who has worked so long and so hard to become.

High-Gain Insights

 It's easy to agree on the importance of focusing on people about whom we care, projects we want to complete, goals we want to achieve, our careers, and our health. With so many interruptions and distractions at work and in our lives, we've no choice but to prioritize the few things that are really important.

Focus is a good beginning, but we then must follow through. It's in following through where the map we made turns into the road trip we actually take. Don't be an armchair traveler. Be clear. Persevere. Act. Celebrate.

Your knowledge of what's truly important to you is critical to your ability to focus and finish. Bringing conversations and projects to conclusion creates deep personal satisfaction and raises your influence as well as your credibility with others.

When interviewed about her success on court, tennis star Jennifer Capriati said, "You have to block everything out and be extremely focused, and be relaxed and mellow, too." So how do you pull all that together under pressure? It's not easy, but following are some strategies you can use.

First, list the top seven major tasks or projects you are responsible for accomplishing at work. Rank the projects according to their importance. That is, which will have the greatest impact.

Task/Project	Rank by Importance

Pick one task or project upon which you want to focus and finish. What can (and will) you do differently so you can focus more effectively than ever on this task or project?

What are the key steps that, when you truly focus, will drive the task/project to the finish line?

_____

_____

_____

Prioritize, focus, and finish at home and in your personal life. List the top five goals or projects you have at home or personal goals you want to achieve, and rank the projects according to their importance.

Task/Project	Rank by Importance

Pick one goal or project upon which you want to focus and finish. What can (and will) you do differently so you can focus more effectively than ever?

What are the key steps that, when you truly focus, will drive your goal/project to the finish line?

_____

_____

_____

"A person who aims at nothing is sure to hit it."

– ANONYMOUS

"It's a funny thing about life; if you refuse to accept anything but the best, you very often get it."

– W. SOMERSET MAUGHAM

"What we call luck, what we call chance, is what happens when preparation meet opportunity.

– WILL SMITH

CHAPTER 12
Find Joy

A Toy Poodle by the name of Ruby lives in our neighborhood. Ruby is a special dog. She almost died a few years ago when she was attacked by an Akita. The perpetrator had Ruby's head in his mouth with such a tight grip that it popped one of her eyes out of its socket. Luckily, Ruby's eye was saved and so was Ruby, although she lost the sight in that eye. Ruby's spirit, however, remained undiminished.

Ruby's proud owners – Julie, Andrew, and their daughter Maria – always think of Ruby as a medical miracle, but she's even more special than that. Whenever Ruby is taking a walk and meets another person or another dog on the street, she gets so excited that she jumps up in the air and spins round and round and round. It's an amazing sight and a delight to behold. Once she's done spinning, she lies down flat on her back so dogs can sniff her. She does this even after the Akita, a dog she did not know, nearly killed her.

Scout loves her and can hardly wait to see her on our walks. When we're in our front yard and Ruby walks by, Scout can barely contain his wagging tail and his whines of joy. He remains focused on her. I have to tell him to stay because he looks like he's getting ready to bolt through our hidden-fence system to greet his friend.

No one taught Ruby these tricks. They just came to her naturally. I'm not sure what Ruby did in her previous life, but I'd be willing to bet it had something to do with bringing great joy to everyone who crossed her path. She is an incomparable walking celebration of life.

Paul's Story

 People could learn a lot from a dog like Ruby when it comes to expressing joy, but if Ruby had a human counterpart, it would be Paul.

Paul has run an advertising agency for many years. He recently sold his company to his leadership team. Bill has become CEO, and Paul is staying on as Chairman. Paul has left his mark on the agency. Around the community, he's known for his high values and generous ways. And he's created the kind of culture in which people want to work. By his own acknowledgement, Paul's an eternal optimist. He looks at life and business through a positive lens. Here are some of his tenets:

- The glass is always half full.
- Every "no" is a step closer to a "yes."
- Life is what you make it.
- Luck is what happens when opportunities meet preparation.
- Opportunities are like plants, they must be nurtured with water and sunshine and an occasional weeding.
- Win and lose gracefully.
- Make mistakes, but learn from them.
- Try new things and accept failure as a small price.

Paul celebrates life and brings an atmosphere of festivity to his firm. In the advertising business, people work really hard to deliver on client deadlines. Working around the clock is not unusual. So Paul and his team feel it's important to reward and acknowledge people and their efforts. ˙

Paul and Bill do a lot to celebrate their people, and they have a lot to celebrate. They've become a successful and well-respected agency over the years.

Paul Knows How to Celebrate (In His Own Words)

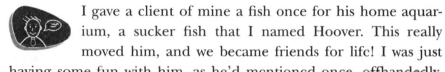 I gave a client of mine a fish once for his home aquarium, a sucker fish that I named Hoover. This really moved him, and we became friends for life! I was just having some fun with him, as he'd mentioned once, offhandedly, that the aquarium was his favorite hobby. Now he's on our board of directors and talks about that fish to this day.

We used to have an annual year-end bonus system that was kind of taken for granted. It became sort of expected after a while, not terribly motivating. Twelve years ago we changed this to a quarterly "carrot bonus" system that brings the rewards closer to the activity that produces results. For the first three quarters of this program, we paid no bonuses. But since then we've paid forty-five consecutive carrot bonuses.

A carrot bonus is a reward system that pays bonuses based on achieving certain goals. If you reach the goal, you get the bonus. The closer the reward is to the goal, the more motivating the program. Quarterly bonuses are a good idea because frequent payouts keep the "carrot" in the forefront of participants' minds on a daily basis.

We celebrate each one in our monthly company-wide "Muffin Meeting," where we all gather for an hour or so to discuss company news. Usually, we also celebrate each carrot with a special all-company party or event held at a local pub with snacks, games, booze, and camaraderie. Sometimes the senior execs make small speeches, sometimes not. We celebrate new account wins with champagne, beer, and pizza. We celebrate each new employee with a first-day Bagel Breakfast introduction in our main lobby. Of course, we have an annual holiday party for ourselves and our spouses, but we also hold a special holiday party for our clients to celebrate those valuable relationships.

In addition, the agency president annually gives "President's Awards" to meritorious people below the senior level. These are typically $1,000 to $3,000 cash bonuses, and may also include a travel award or spa treatment, for example, as a way to celebrate terrific effort during the year. This award can go deep into the company, to the lowest staffing levels.

We hold a once-a-month company lunch where our COO and CEO slap on aprons and chef hats and dish out free food to everyone. And we annually honor about five to six employees with Iron Achievement awards for effort and results, Hallmark awards for character and professionalism, and Vision awards for creative excellence.

In addition to what we do for our own staff, sometimes we invite clients to join the celebrations. Once, a hard-to-please client came over to speak with the agency team that handled his account. He handed them small cash checks, shook each hand, and treated them to beer and wings. It had a marvelous affect on the team.

One time a client asked my predecessor, Walt, out to lunch in December and handed him a check for $25,000! Walt never asked for it – it was just a token of his esteem and appreciation for our superb efforts and results for them that year. Walt literally cried; tears rolled down his cheeks. Think about how special that must have been. Imagine the loyalty it engendered. Incredible! Just <u>incredible!</u>

High-Gain Insights

 Regardless of your position or job title at work, you can make it your business to catch somebody doing something right. And when you do, you can celebrate them with positive feedback. There are always ways to make people feel good about their accomplishments.

Your commitment to, and practice of, acknowledging and affirming small, positive steps will add up to big wins. Without rewards and reinforcement, people will not be able to sustain difficult and challenging efforts with energy, enthusiasm, and effectiveness.

Oprah Winfrey said, "The more you praise and celebrate your life, the more there is in life to celebrate." Celebration feeds upon celebration.

Following are some Practical Ideas that may help.

Select one or two of these ideas and integrate them into your work (and life!):

- Give yourself and others small gifts for work well done.

- Use humor, unusual presents, and surprises to keep it fresh.

- Smile and offer encouragement more, especially when others are feeling "under the gun."

- Give yourself or others time off (or some other reward) after completing a major project that required a lot of extra energy or time.

- Keep your "praise ratio" high – that is, praise people seven to ten times for every one challenge, correction, or critique.

"More than anything else, dogs are creatures of play, whose spontaneous interaction with life bespeaks their goodness."
— The Monks of New Skeet, *I & Dog*

CHAPTER 13

Become an Encouraging Presence

Remember the Flintstones and how Dino the dog-dinosaur greeted Fred? Dino was so overcome with joy to see Fred walk in the door that he'd literally knock Fred over, sit on Fred's stomach, and lick his face. Scout's not exactly like that (he's much smaller than Dino), but when I walk in the door at home, I'm greeted by a running, rollicking, white ball of fur with a single mission: to welcome me home. I'm sniffed, kissed, and licked like a long-lost friend.

For me, there's no place like home at the end of a long, hard day. I get dinner started and change out of my work clothes. Scout bounds upstairs to our bedroom after me and curls up on the couch there. He'll wait until I'm done and ready to return to the kitchen.

During dinner, Scout lies next to us at the table and eats his food. It's been sitting out all day, but he waits for us. Bob, our dog trainer, says Bichons are social animals, and they don't like to eat alone. Scout is pretty much glued to my ankle during this time, following my every move.

Scout is an encouraging presence. I feel his energy. "Connect," he seems to be saying. "Stay close. Pet me."

On the weekend, Scout is always a joy to be around. Whether napping on the floor next to us when we relax in the family room, playing with one of his toys in the house, or on our outdoor walks together, he is happy and ready for affection.

Scout doesn't learn anything from being scolded. I should have known this from my experiences with human beings. Ninety-three percent of communications is relayed by tone and body language, and seven percent is through the spoken word.[2] On the rare occasions I've yelled at Scout, when I've discovered that he's urinated in the house, for example, he cowers and looks confused. He doesn't look like he understands what I'm saying, but he surely reacts to my harsh tone and serious facial expressions. He probably wonders what's wrong with his crazy human housemate.

Becoming an encouraging leader for Scout wasn't a natural talent for me; it was a skill I had to learn and am still learning. Bob has taught me so much about how to train and encourage Scout through positive modeling. And Scout has taught me about the power of encouragement through how quickly he responds to positive and clear direction.

So I've learned that the only way to train Scout is through encouragement and gentle corrections. I use a lot of "Good boy!"s. I pet him and offer him treats to let him know when he's done something well. I try to catch him in the act of doing something right, and then I praise him.

Scout helps turn our house into a home. He's like his own fireplace, hot cup of cocoa, and stuffed animal all rolled into one. Scout *is* an encouraging presence. He didn't have to learn how to be one, as I did.

I decided to attend a leadership program a colleague was running. It was a week-long program that gave me time and space to think about my leadership style. Away from the office, away from the hectic pace, out in the country, it was a welcome retreat, and I knew

---

[2]Research by Albert Mehrabian

I needed to work on becoming an encouraging presence, which would be my focus at this workshop.

I took a number of insight-generating instruments in advance of the seminar. One in particular I had taken a couple of times before. The results once again indicated that my people skills – my ability to influence people in a positive and encouraging way – remained on the low end of the rating scale.

I began to think about the implications of this for me in my life and my work. It's not as if I hadn't heard it before, but this time it hit me at a different level. Our firm was growing. I'm a leadership developer. So I asked myself, "How would my effectiveness in my marriage and my parenting, in co-running the firm, and in my work with clients rise if I could figure out how to elevate my encouraging presence?"

I questioned myself in all aspects of my life:

Have I been as encouraging to my husband and my children as I could have been?

How have I been discouraging to them?

Have I been as encouraging to my business partner and our staff as I might have been?

How have I been affecting our clients? Was I too intense? Have I encouraged them enough?

I concluded that I hadn't been encouraging enough on a consistent basis, in all areas of my life and work, and I wanted to change that. I took a look at how I was interacting with people when I was calm and when I was under stress. I had been focusing a lot on the tasks at hand and getting things done, but hadn't spent enough time focusing on the people and giving them a positive experience. That was what had to change.

So when I returned home, I made a commitment to consciously change the equation. I elevated people to a level higher than the task at hand. Every time I met with anyone, I set out two goals for myself in this order: 1) Make a meaningful connection and give the person a positive experience. 2) Work on the subject matter at hand.

My demeanor changed as soon as I decided that I wanted to relate more positively to people. I was less serious. I smiled more. I relaxed more. I made sure to encourage people more. I really started to connect.

One of the things I had to change, in particular, was the way I approached solving problems. In the past, when a problem came up, I felt it was my job to solve it. I approached problems with an urgency that intensified the problem and didn't feel good to people.

Now I've put problems into a better perspective; they don't seem as urgent. I rely more on other people to help solve them. I trust their judgment. I'm less anxious. I've let go a bit. Now people react more to the problem and less to me. I believe that to become an encouraging presence involves acting on three principles:

1. Dedicate yourself to developing the people in your life at work and at home – it is the highest form of respect and surest way to get peak performance.

2. Make it safe for people to speak truthfully.

3. Learn to regulate your emotions and recognize the impact you have on people.

I worked on managing my emotions first. The best leaders hear what they need to know because they make it safe for people to tell them. Our team communicates well. We say what we need to say to each other even if it's difficult. We're all grateful for it.

My next area of focus was to spend more regularly scheduled time developing our people.

My husband and my business partner have commented on the positive changes in me. They've told me it's been easier and more fun to interact with me. They've encouraged me to continue my work. I recently took that insight-generating test again, just to see if I'd made any progress on paper. As it turned out, my people-skills score almost doubled.

The Incredible Father Jim

 Father Jim leads one of the best-attended churches in our area. He is an old friend of my business partner, Jim Ramerman. I've gotten to know Father Jim over the past ten years. He's a very unique and special man.

Jim once told me, "When you're with Father Jim, you feel like you're the center of his world and his good friend all rolled into one."

With his full eye contact and complete focus, you feel the energy of his positive connection, and he makes you feel as if the world has momentarily stopped. Everyone loves Father Jim and wants to be around him. After services, there's often a line of parishioners waiting to greet him. This doesn't rush Father Jim one bit. He talks to people one at a time and gives each person his full attention. It's no wonder that he's a popular man.

Father Jim has some amazing talents, too. He remembers your name, your birthday, your anniversary, the anniversary of deaths in your family, and the anniversary of your first date. Wow! It's simply amazing!

When he was in college, he and his classmates couldn't afford cars of their own, so Father Jim suggested a group of them pool their limited funds. They bought a Studebaker together, shared the expenses of maintaining the car, and set up a driving schedule. It taught them about compromising and resolving conflicts and working as a team toward a shared goal. Father Jim has never forgotten that lesson. He's living his dream and helping others to live theirs. His mission is to reach out to the poor and help make their lives better. He changes the world and our community one person at a time.

Father Jim sees possibilities where others see problems. When he came to his church it was on the verge of bankruptcy. They needed money just to keep the lights turned on. Instead of saving every penny, he decided to tithe money to the poor, who needed it more. With that kind of optimistic leadership at the helm, the parish began to grow. They grew from 150 members to more than 3,000 members. Now they attract people from all walks of life, particularly those who have felt disenfranchised from traditional churches.

He has helped people get married whose hearts have been broken. He has helped people start businesses who didn't think they could. He has helped people change their lives because he believes in them. And he has helped people believe in themselves.

Father Jim gives the lives he touches a total, positive regard. It's his gift. It's a rare talent. I know Father Jim will continue his work, and he needs no encouragement, because he's got enough for all of us.

High-Gain Insights

 Increasing your encouraging presence isn't just a nice thing to do; it helps make work more fun and you and the people around you more productive. An encouraging presence also makes it possible for you to become more effective by increasing your ability to positively influence people. While some people seem to have more of a natural ability to be encouraging, anyone can do it.

Your attitude has a great impact on others. For others to have a positive attitude, start with ensuring that you have a positive attitude yourself. Most importantly, you must have a hopeful, affirming view of those you want to encourage.

Your tone of voice is three times more powerful than the words you say. Your nonverbal messages are six times more powerful than the words you say. Your words and your nonverbal messages must be congruent.

The effective encourager motivates through the optimal balance and timing of positive feedback and challenge. In general, eight out of ten feedback messages should be positive and illuminate the specific positive behaviors and the positive results they generated. In other words, "Catch them doing something right!"

I've heard a number of people in leadership positions suggest that people know what you think of them by what you ask of them. Give others challenges that are significant and achievable. Tell them why you asked them – why their skills and talents are a fit for the assignment. Help them, but don't take over. Celebrate when they reach their goals.

Find out what uniquely motivates each individual and adjust your rewards system to that particular set of motivators.

Commit time to those you seek to encourage. Your time, your very best presence, and your positive attitude greatly motivate others.

Following are some Practical Ideas that may help you become a more encouraging presence.

- Keep this page on your desk as a guide.
- Get a screen saver that will remind you to be an encouraging presence – a sunset, rainbow, picture of your role model for positive energy (JFK, Oprah, etc.).
- Make sure that everyone on your team knows that people skills are important. (Encouragement may be part of your performance evaluation.)
- Keep a bowl of candy – a kind you love and enjoy – and share it with everyone as a reminder to keep joy present and incorporate it into your personality.

CHAPTER 14
Find Your Knack for Leadership

Erin, a member of our team at work, tells a great story about her childhood dog, Libby, a Golden Retriever.

When Erin was a little girl, she and her parents sometimes ate dinner in front of the television. Libby displayed different behavior around each person's food. The dog would never touch Erin's father's dish. Erin's dad was the alpha male. If her father got up during his meal and left his dish on the floor, Libby wouldn't touch it.

Libby wouldn't bother Erin's mother's dish either, as long as she was eating. But if she left the room, the dog would eat the food on her plate. And Erin? Libby would often try to eat Erin's food right off the plate while it was in her hands, and she could never leave her plate unattended because the food would be gone when she got back.

Dogs know who's in charge and how to work the system. My dog, Scout, is no different.

Scout Gets a Bath

Scout has never questioned Terry's leadership. Terry snaps his fingers, and Scout comes from anywhere in the house, at any time, for any reason. It doesn't work quite that way for me, especially when I'm trying to give Scout a bath.

On most Saturday mornings, I groom Scout. I brush him, bathe him in the kitchen sink, and blow him dry on the kitchen table. I keep his bath towels and shampoo under the kitchen sink for easy access. The whole process takes about an hour.

The ritual begins with me putting on my apron. Scout senses what's coming next as soon as that happens. He'll watch me carefully from a safe distance and begin to back up into the family room, and then he turns and dashes out his doggie door. When he's safely on the outside deck, he sticks his neck through the doggie door to see if the coast is clear, then he hightails it for his crate, bypassing me and the dreaded bath.

I've had to come up with all kinds of tricks to make sure he doesn't bolt out the doggie door anymore: I close the doggie door first, I don't put on my apron until he's in the sink, or I wait until he's in the sink before taking out all the supplies. I eventually corral him, at which point he has no choice but to submit.

After the bath comes the blow dry. Bichons are furry white puff-balls when they are fully coiffed. I don't go for the show-dog look, but I do like a nicely brushed, sweet-smelling Scout. So with Scout on the kitchen table and the hairdryer in my hand, I dry and brush him until he's in great shape. He sits for drying and brushing without much resistance, except for his occasional pacing back and forth on the table.

Wrestling Scout into his bath is one of the places my leadership still gets tested, but I'm finding my way. I have to admit that once in a while I break down and ask Terry for his help. As you might guess, all he does is snap his fingers, Scout comes, and I put him in the sink for his bath. I guess I still have a battle or two to wage before I win the war.

The Upside of Risk Taking

 Karen had a few things to learn about leadership when she started working with her new company. Her new position entailed supervising thirty administrative people with a variety of experience and tenure.

She had moved to a new part of the city for this position. She'd bought a new condominium and hadn't yet closed on the deal when she joined our management-development program. For Karen, her new position as an administrative manager was a step up in responsibilities from jobs she held in the past. She had supervised people before, but not this many.

It didn't take Karen long to begin to doubt whether she could handle her new job. Her boss, Tina, with whom she had a good relationship, recently let her know that the company was consolidating some functions and accelerating its growth plans for the year. This would mean that Karen would be taking on a second administrative group of similar size by the end of the year.

Tina had a lot of confidence in Karen, but also realized that Karen's "softer" management style might present a challenge for her. In order to manage two groups, Karen would have to make decisions faster and handle more complex situations. Tina knew Karen would have concerns about the new plans, so she suggested Karen work with me.

I invited Karen to some group development meetings with her peers, and then we met for an individual coaching session. I started by asking her if I could give her some blunt feedback. (Although Karen had contracted me for feedback throughout the program, I've always felt it's important to ask.) Karen readily agreed.

"I notice that in the group meetings, you go out of your way to be nice to your colleagues, you facilitate their participation, but you rarely let the group know what you think. Are you aware that's happening?" I asked.

"Hmmm," Karen began, smiling, thinking about it. She was being nice to me, too.

"I'm kind of new in the group. I'm still feeling my way. It's important to me that people are comfortable with me, and that I'm comfortable with them."

"Do you want to be comfortable and keep people comfortable, or do you want to grow and help people grow?" I asked her.

She sat up in her chair, a bit taken aback by my directness, but then she responded. "I'd like to be comfortable *and* grow. Why do they have to be mutually exclusive? I don't like a lot of controversy. I think we should let sleeping dogs lie."

It was a brisk day outside, but our office was warm. I noticed that Karen crossed her arms in front of her as if she had a chill.

"You're not going to get much out of this program unless you take some risks," I told her. "And speaking of risks, taking on a second department is a heck of risk to manage."

"I'm not a great risk-taker. In fact, I'll be honest with you . . . I just don't like taking risks at all. But I did take one recently that paid off. I'm proud of myself. Can I tell you about it?"

"Sure."

"I was running a meeting recently with my peers, and Tina was in the room. She asked if she could change something on the agenda at the last minute. The group's time together was short, and we all had ample input time in constructing the agenda. Although I wanted to accommodate her and I was afraid she might get angry with me if I didn't, I said 'no' because it would have been disrespectful to the group to bump one of their agenda items."

"What was Tina's reaction?" I asked.

"She said it was fine," Karen replied.

"In your mind, what's at risk when you say 'no' to Tina or to a colleague?"

"I'm afraid that if I have a confrontation, people could get angry or frustrated with me."

"Then what?" I asked.

"If they get angry with me, they might see me negatively and my relationship with them could be jeopardized."

"Then what?"

"Then I could be unhappy working for the company," Karen said hesitantly. "And the company could be unhappy with me."

"Then what?"

"Then I could decide to leave, I suppose, or they could fire me. Either would be an unpleasant change."

We both let the last statement hang in silence for a moment.

Karen spoke first. "I guess I didn't realize how deep my feelings went on this one."

I wanted to encourage her to keep going.

"What are some other feelings you might be having and not sharing?"

"I've been wondering whether I'm right for this job. Taking on this new department has made me nervous."

"Do you want to succeed at this new level of responsibility that's being presented to you?" I asked her, hoping she'd dig deeper.

"Yes, I think so," she said halfheartedly.

"Do you think Tina would have given you this position and this development opportunity if she wasn't confident in your abilities?"

"No. Tina knows I can do it."

"Then you'll need to be hungry and kick up your leadership skills. You'll need to become more comfortable with being uncomfortable if you want to grow. And you'll need to stop playing it safe." I said all of this slowly and deliberately, hoping that it would sink in.

Then I asked, "How would doing these things benefit you and your department?"

I noticed her arms had uncrossed.

Karen said, "I would be more confident. I would be more assertive. I would make better decisions. And I would take more risks."

"You'd be a leader," I suggested. "Do you know who Larry Bird is?"

"Sure. I love basketball. Larry Bird was a great player for the Boston Celtics."

I nodded, told Karen that was exactly right, and then shared with her one of Larry Bird's remarkable quotes that I had written down in preparation for our meeting:

"Leadership is getting players to believe in you. If you tell a teammate you're ready to play as tough as you're able to, you'd better go out there and do it. Players will see right through a phony. And they can tell when you're not giving it all you've got. Leadership is diving for a loose ball, getting the crowd involved, getting other players involved. It's being able to take it as well as dish it out. That's the only way you're going to get respect from the players."

I let her think about that for a while, and then I asked her if that's the kind of greatness to which she aspired.

"Yes, I want to become a leader," she said, this time with conviction.

"Then how can you get started at the next group meeting?" I asked.

Karen gave it some thought, and then she said that, for starters, she would disclose what she had learned about herself at this session. Second, she would increase her participation level on whatever subject came up at the next meeting.

And she did. Just like that. She made it look easy, although we both knew it wasn't.

The group applauded her disclosures and supported her efforts. She consciously participated throughout the meeting and joked back and forth with her colleagues in a more confident voice and a higher level of repartee. She wasn't quite as nice, but she was honest, and that was a good thing for Karen's growth.

As for the new department, Karen's taking it one day at a time. She's receiving excellent guidance from Tina and plenty of support from her peers.

Karen is making sound business decisions, taking managed risks, and feeling more and more confident each day.

Most important, she has found her knack for leadership. And it becomes her.

High-Gain Insights

 Everyone can become more of a leader. Leadership is a discipline that can be learned, and over the years I've enjoyed watching people from all walks of life rise to their leadership potential.

To find your knack for leadership, you first have to desire to be a leader (or more of a leader). Where is it that you want to have more of a positive influence? At work? At home? Ask yourself how much you want to change, how much energy you want to invest, and how "comfortable you can become with discomfort" in order to find or develop, your knack. Then commit. Now you're ready to make some shifts to becoming a more effective leader. Here are some Practical Ideas that may help.

Envisioning is a tool that professional athletes use to great success. Tiger Woods pictures winning more major golf titles than Jack Nicklaus. He also envisions his ball landing in the fairway, not the water, and going in the cup, not "rimming out."

1. Put a picture of a leader you admire clearly in your mind (such as Larry Bird, Jack Welch, Lincoln, etc.).

2. What is their attitude? Their philosophy of life and leadership? How do they handle challenges?

3. Consider the situations at work that test your leadership where you need to find your knack. Imagine yourself handling it with the energy, confidence, and finesse of your admired leader. Now envision how you will handle it: the moves and actions you will take, who you will talk to, and how. Envision it going well, very well.

4. Picture challenges where it doesn't go well at all, and envision yourself bouncing back, persevering, and applying your new knack for leadership.

"Life is like a dogsled race – if you ain't the lead dog, the scenery never changes."

– LEWIS GRIZZARD

CHAPTER 15
Become "Change-Able"

I conducted a session in the Southwest on building high-performance teams with thirty engineering managers from across the country. They all worked for an international engineering firm.

Ethan was the vice president of an engineering-services department. He had been in the position for just under a year, and was challenged to convince his managers to change their mindsets. Ethan wanted to convert from individual stand-alone offices (servicing clients solely in their regions) to thinking like a team and sharing work across the country. He believed this would provide fuller services, assure timely delivery, and initiate a higher quality of work among their teams.

The firm put a bonus system in place as an incentive to managers, but performance was still lagging across the firm, and Ethan wanted to understand and fix the issues.

Ethan also told me that the managers tended toward the quiet side and had not received much formal development in management skills in the past. They were good, solid, technically trained people, and many had been with the firm a long time.

I wondered what the barriers to change in this group might be and whether the group would be ready to acknowledge them at the upcoming meeting, especially with Ethan in the room. Change was never easy in any organization, and I hoped that Ethan would have reasonable expectations of the group's first run at this. I prepared myself for a day of potential revelation and the possibility that the managers might resist the effort, using whatever fear of change they might have as a blocker.

The managers and I met for the first time at the meeting. I opened the day by setting the goals as open and honest conversation and speaking the truth. I set up confidentiality norms and told the quiet folks that I would draw them out and asked the talkative ones not to dominate discussions. With good ground rules in place, people began to relax early and got ready to focus on the task at hand.

We began the day by reviewing an instrument all thirty had taken in advance of the meeting. The DISC instrument is well-known and we've used it many times. It provided a lot of insight for the group on how they drive for results on tasks, how they value relationships, how they manage change, and how they comply with rules.

The managers shared remarkably similar characteristics. The majority of the group seemed task-driven and wanted to follow the rules. As a group, they were also low on relationship skills and didn't appreciate change.

One person asked only half-jokingly, "Are all engineers this boring?"

"No two engineers are alike," I answered diplomatically. "But that doesn't mean you can't relate to each other more effectively and learn to like change. We just have to find a way for each of you to become more change-friendly by going about it in the right way and at the right pace for this group."

The room was large and set up in a horseshoe shape so we could all see each other easily. I remember thinking that the atmosphere in the room was a bit chilly at the start. But as the group opened up to each other, the room seemed to warm.

The managers were fascinated by the results of the DISC instrument. They chuckled at their similarities and differences and began to understand how teaming might be a challenge for a group with these characteristics. As the day went on, the newly forming team began to dig deeper into the barriers that could be getting in the way of making some important changes. They began to loosen up with each other and began, as well, to share their insecurities and the impact their behaviors were having on each other.

One manager took a risk and said, "I'm a pretty competitive guy. I like doing things myself, and it's important that my office staff feels like winners. We like servicing our clients directly."

"I'm curious," Ethan said. "Doesn't the new bonus system help you think about teaming with each other more?"

"Not really," another replied, "I'd rather have the work done right by my people in my own office, even if I mess up once in a while. I do procrastinate at times about calling the client if we're going to miss a deadline. But I'd rather take those consequences and keep control."

"How many of the rest of you feel that way?" I asked. Most of the people in the room raised their hands. Ethan was visibly perplexed. He thought the bonus would have been a motivator for the managers. Discovering that it didn't have the impact he had hoped was a key moment for Ethan. But he was to learn more, much more about this team before the day was over.

The managers discovered that while collectively they had good customer focus and senior-level support, they were lacking in decision-making and clarity on assignments, their execution as a team was poor, and trust among team members was low.

Another manager began to reveal more.

"Hey," he said to the group, "with all due respect, when I have sent work over to some of you guys, you've screwed it up. Sometimes when we work on other projects together, you don't follow through and get it done. How am I supposed to trust you? When that kind of stuff happens, I pull back into my own office and stop teaming."

I saw a lot of heads nodding yes. It looked like several managers had the same experience. Now we were getting closer to the barriers that were preventing this group from becoming a team.

The managers divided into small groups to tackle each issue and reported back on potential solutions. Each breakout group went at it. You could feel their energy rising as they stood at the easels and prepared their suggestions. Engaged. Focused. Talkative. Suggestions flying. It was clear that this well-intentioned group of dedicated people wanted to find answers just as much as Ethan did.

Here is some of what they discovered through their hard work and open and revealing dialogue:

1. Poor execution between the engineering managers was driven by a lack of trust among team members.

2. Trust among team members was low because commitments on delivering work and finishing projects were not honored.

3. Delivery dates and promises slipped because of poor time management and a lack of priority-setting.

4. Priorities lost focus because the group didn't delegate to their staff well.

5. Delegation didn't happen because the managers didn't trust their people to do the work as well as they could do it. They feared their people would make mistakes that would reflect poorly on them as managers. If others did a good job, they wouldn't be needed and would consequently lose their jobs. And they weren't sure how to step up and take on new responsibilities.

And more insights followed. They feared taking on new levels of responsibility that were being requested of them by the VP, because they lacked the confidence that they could learn new things. This lack of confidence stemmed from their perception that the firm wasn't investing in their development as managers up until now. They never had the chance to demonstrate to themselves or the firm that they could learn how to grow and change.

<u>Wow!</u> I looked around the room. Everyone was looking at the easel that displayed what they had known deep down. It was as if a group epiphany had taken place. If a thought bubble could have appeared above their heads, it might have read, "So that's why we've been feeling so uneasy about all these new expectations!"

The risk these managers took to dig deeper and reveal the root causes paid off. They had their own reasons for not changing, but they'd never expressed them. Now that the issues were on the table, they didn't look so scary anymore. Each could be addressed through an ongoing development effort that Ethan was willing to support.

High-Gain Insights

 Is your organization undergoing change? Do you think change could increase your performance or the performance of your entire team? Get on the front end of the curve. Ask yourself the following questions:

- What about change excites me? Why?

- What about change scares me? Why?

- What are the benefits and risks of the change?

- What is my role in the change?

- What can I do to get ready for change?

- How will I have to change?

- What is the risk of changing?

- What is the risk of not changing?

- What are some specific changes I want to make?

Here are some Practical Ideas that may help you cope with change:

1. After considering the questions above, get clear on one change you're committed to make (make sure it's doable and desirable).

2. Fall in love with (or at least "make friends with") the change you are going to make. The fear of change is a huge fear for many, many people!

3. Build personal commitment. Write down the change you are going to make, what it will look like when you've made it, the steps along the way, as well as the time and resources you'll need. Writing down goals significantly increases the likelihood of them becoming a reality.

4. Make a public commitment and get support. Tell others who are supportive about the change you are going to make. Give them permission to remind, encourage, and challenge you to stay the course.

5. Take the first step – put your change plan into action. Repeat it as often as possible so you can turn the change into a habit.

Once your new behavior is integrated into your life, you can tackle the next change, and the next. You will become changeable.

"What separates the winners from the losers is how a person reacts to each new twist of fate."

– DONALD TRUMP

CHAPTER 16

Find Meaning in Your Work

I was sitting at an outdoor plaza in Santa Barbara, California when I met Logan, a Collie, for the first time. I couldn't look away from him. He was regal, handsome, and seemed very approachable and gentle. I introduced myself to his owner, Myron, and asked if his dog liked people.

"He *loves* people!" Myron replied. So I asked if I could pet Logan and Myron said, "Of course."

That was the beginning of our friendship. Later that evening, at my brother's wedding, in walked Myron and his wife, Vicki. We recognized each other immediately and couldn't help but laugh. Neither one of us knew that we were both going to be at my brother's wedding. As it turned out, Logan had played a big part in Myron and Vicki meeting lots of new people. When I asked them if they were willing to be interviewed (on Logan's behalf) for my book, they were thrilled.

Vicki: Logan weighs eighty-five pounds. He's a Rough Collie (meaning long-haired), and he's a tri. That means his color is mostly black, with a white ruff and tan markings on his face. His full name is Paragon San Francisco Nights, and he earned the title of "Champion" from The Collie Club of America in 1999 at the age of six.

Myron: When Logan was a puppy, Vicki and I kissed him good-bye and sent him to a camp for six months to be trained in his show skills – stance, handling, temperament, affability with other dogs, and so on – at a home in Berkeley, California, with five other Collies in training. Logan loved his training. Took to it right away, like he was born to it. He let his handlers touch him and work with him and never got upset.

Vicki: At the camp, all of the doors where they housed the dogs were Dutch doors, you know the kind, with the bottoms closed and the tops open so the dogs could see each other. They understood that dogs were social animals. The dogs were trained as a pack to follow a leader. As one of their exercises, the trainer would slowly drive his motorcycle down the street with the Collies running alongside him on the sidewalk. If any Collie broke from the pack, the leader would stop his motorcycle and send the Collie back to the group. Logan loved this exercise.

Myron: Logan also loved to compete in dog shows, and he competed many times between the ages of three and six. With his handler, he glided at a perfect pace. Alert. Ears up. Focused. Tail popped. Eyes straight ahead. He won a lot of titles. When he won, he jumped straight up in the air with excitement and kissed his handler. One time he even kissed one of the judges during the competition.

Vicki: Everyone loves Logan and Logan loves his work.

I thought that was an interesting comment, so I asked Vicki and Myron what they felt Logan's work was.

Myron: "Well, I've never been asked to put it into words before. That makes it a good question, I suppose. He's a former champion and a fine companion, for sure. But I think Logan's deeper work is to bring out the best in people of all kinds and to connect people that wouldn't have connected under any other circumstance."

Vicki: "Yes, that's true. I would agree with that. When I walk down the street with Logan, the world calls out to him from all directions. Locals. Tourists. People in cars. Complete strangers. Even homeless people. A man named McCoy, who lives on the streets, has taken a particular liking to our Logan. Every day on our walks, McCoy waits at the coffee shop to see him. When Logan comes up to him, McCoy hugs him, holds him, and watches him for me when I go into the shop to buy my coffee. When I come out, I'll sit and talk with McCoy for a while."

Myron: "I've met McCoy on some of Logan's walks. He's a great guy. We've developed a special bond because of Logan."

Vicki and Myron have since told me that Logan continues his special work in his retirement. He smiles his gentle smile. He stands in his regal stance. He walks down the street with his head held high. He continues to introduce Vicki and Myron to people they wouldn't have otherwise met. And he continues to touch people in meaningful ways, including me. I owe my relationship with Vicki and Myron to Logan.

Logan has helped Myron and Vicki find joy and meaning in their lives, but not everyone is so lucky. Not too long ago, I was with an old friend, and we were catching up on our lives. She stopped working to stay at home and raise her boys after a long career in a school system. Her husband, Theodore, known to his friends as "Big Ted," had worked hard to build his law firm and now ran a large operation. My friend said he was doing really *well*.

When I asked her what she meant by "well," she said, in a not-too-enthusiastic voice, "You know, *financially*."

I then asked her if Big Ted liked his work. She said no, he spent most of his time supervising people now rather than practicing law, which he wasn't so hot about. I kept pressing her, and she grew more and more uncomfortable with our conversation.

Finally she said, "He's lost his connection to his work. He used to have a passion for it. He used to love the law. Now he doesn't really get a chance to spend any time with it anymore."

*   *   *

I love the story about the man who was sweeping the floor at NASA, the space agency. When asked what he did for a living, he replied, "I sent a man to the moon." I don't know if the story is true, but the point is well-taken. So many people with whom I talk have lost their connection with and love for their work: supervisors, managers, vice presidents, and CEOs. Some people love their work, but they're unhappy with their work environment, or the pressure, or the hours. *CNN/Money* published a survey a couple of years ago revealing that eight out of ten Americans want a new job. Some people make a lot of money at jobs they don't love anymore, or they work at a pace that's literally killing them. Some people don't feel they are paid enough and don't like how hard they are expected to work. Approximately 7.5 million Americans currently work at least two jobs.

If you can't make a meaningful connection with what you're doing anymore, and you have no choice but to work, and you don't feel empowered to make a change, you can start to feel trapped. Perhaps you're not seeing the choices available to you.

Edmund Burke once said, "We must all obey the great law of change. It is the most powerful law of nature." I believe that's true.

You may have a harder time maintaining a deeper connection with your work because of what I call "organizational static." Organizational static is the issues, people, conflicts, competing priorities, and all the things that get in the way of remembering why you love your job and why it's important. Static can be disorienting and can pull you in negative directions if you let it.

Here are the top three examples of organizational static I've heard over the years:

1. The big guns can't agree, so I'll wait till they figure it out.

2. This place is so chaotic and disorganized that nothing seems to get done, so why should I push it?

3. The company doesn't care about quality anymore, so why should I?

You might also unknowingly bring attitudes or barriers along with you that make it harder to find the kind of meaningful connection to work that I've been talking about. For example, here are the top three complaints I've heard people say about their work:

1. "Work is work; it's not supposed to be fun."

2. "I'm bored to death, and I have been for a long time."

3. "I'd love to be doing something else, if I could just figure out how and could afford to make the change."

Since you'll spend so many years of your life working, wouldn't it be great if you could love what you were doing, the people with whom you were doing it, and the organizations for which you were doing it?

You must find a meaningful way to look at work if you want increased satisfaction from your career. To test how you feel about work, picture talking to a trusted friend about your current position:

Best Friend: "What do you do for a living?"
Think about how you would describe your work. What adjectives would you use?

Mom: "How do you like working for your company?"
Think about how you would describe your company. What adjectives would you use?

Significant Other: "How do you like your job?"
What would you say?

UPS Guy: "If you could be anything you wanted, what would it be?"
How would you answer?

The kind of connection I'm talking about is heartfelt. It's a mindset and an attitude; you can't just go through the motions. Here are a few remarkable people I have spoken to who've done it:

- The receptionist in a law firm says she sees her job as brightening people's lives by being kind to them, especially when they have a problem and need her the most.

- An inventor of a car seat for babies says he innovatively redesigned a car seat to save the lives of children after reading the statistics about how many babies die in poorly designed units.

- A manager in a healthcare organization says she raises the health of people in the communities she serves by processing claims accurately and quickly the first time. By keeping quality up and administrative costs down, her job helps insure the uninsured and raises the investment the organization makes in community health efforts.

- Personally, I am dedicated to elevating the practice of leadership and to transforming organizational life in meaningful and progressive ways. That's our firm's mission and my personal pledge. I make this a reality for our clients by seeking root causes of issues, speaking the truth to them, and helping them find the courage to take the right actions at the right time.

Keisha Makes a Change

 I had been working with Keisha for about six months. I began to notice that she was increasingly unhappy at work. She had been managing her department for seven years and she had lost her spark. The job was hard. There were a lot of conflicts in the department, morale was down, and she had been slugging through problem after problem for a long time. It was hard for her to get excited about people, projects, new business, or just about anything anymore.

I raised my concerns and observations with Keisha, and I gave her some examples. She didn't ask a lot of questions in our sessions and didn't seem eager to solve problems. She seemed tentative, unsure of herself. Sometimes she'd have a homework assignment to complete between our meetings, but often she'd come in with it unfinished, and she was late for most of our meetings.

Keisha acknowledged the issues right away. She hadn't said it out loud to anyone, including her husband, but she readily acknowledged she wasn't having fun at work anymore and hadn't for quite some time.

I suggested she consider taking a break from her managerial role. Maybe someone else could fill in for her while she regrouped and re-energized herself. She didn't have to make any long-term decisions until she was ready.

Keisha didn't hesitate. She said she wanted to temporarily step down. She seemed so relieved. A smile returned to her face when she realized she had a way to figure this out without leaving the company. It was the happiest I had seen her in months. Of all the work we'd done together, she said this moment was the most meaningful for her.

Keisha went back to work that afternoon with a mission. She met with her boss and made plans to temporarily step down and to continue working in another capacity for a six-month period. Her boss readily supported her decision.

High-Gain Insights

Life's short. Don't go through the motions at work or in life. It's possible for you, regardless of your position or the company you work for, to find more meaning in your work. You can seek it on your own or with help from others. It's one of the key factors in keeping you happy and focused in the hubbub of organizational life.

Here are some Practical Ideas that may help you find more meaning in your work:

1. Seek to understand the highest-level reason for the existence of the organization. Ask your coworkers what they think. Ask your boss. Check out your organization's mission and vision statements.

2. Ask yourself: Do I believe in the mission? Why? Do I think it's important for the organization to realize its vision? Why?

3. Think about what you do in the organization. How does your job contribute to turning the mission and vision into a reality? Why is your job important? How do you make it special?

4. Write a short, personal work mission statement in your own words that makes the link between what you do and the organization's mission and vision. Read it out loud several times. Put it in a place where you can see it every day to remind yourself.

5. Act in ways that align with the meaning of your personal work mission statements.

A senior staff person at an IT consulting firm was very hesitant to sell his valuable services to clients. I saw the value more than he did until we talked it all the way through and he was able to articulate his value proposition and his personal work mission statement. The following is the statement he came up with:

"I provide systemic IT solutions to the total work processes of my clients' manufacturing firms so that they are optimally efficient to the point where they have a sustainable competitive advantage and are highly profitable."

He also realized he was in the business of "saving" hundreds of jobs and found real meaning that went well beyond the technical focus he once had of his job.

"Beware of a silent dog and still water."

– Latin Proverb

CHAPTER 17

Develop a Great Relationship with Your Boss

Adam and Carrie have done a great job with Jack, their German Shepherd. Adam says their relationship with Jack began like "Internet dating." They saw a picture of Jack on the Internet posted by a "no-kill" shelter on the outskirts of Washington, D.C. From the first time Adam saw Jack's picture he said, "That's the dog I want."

It was love at first sight when they finally met Jack. Jack ran toward Adam and started playing. The shelter interviewed Adam and Carrie to make sure they were suitable for Jack. The other person interested in adopting Jack lived on a houseboat, and that wouldn't have been the best place for an energetic guy like Jack. The deal was done, and Adam and Carrie drove happily off with Jack in their Jeep Wrangler.

Jack didn't bark or whine for the first month in his new home with Carrie and Adam. Jack was timid and slow to open up. My friend BJ, who havens dogs, says that's pretty typical for a dog when he's put into a new situation. She says that for the first thirty days or so, a dog will act like a guest. After that, the dog begins to let down his guard and becomes himself. In Jack's case, not to worry, his bark and his energy were intact.

Adam read up on dog training and did things correctly right from the start. He assumed the alpha role (Carrie assumed the female alpha role) and they taught Jack a few key rules that everyone in the house reinforced:

1. No sitting on the furniture.

2. No lying on the bed.

3. Waiting for permission to go up or down the stairs.

4. Eating after the humans ate. Waiting for permission to eat food out of his bowl or food that was dropped on the floor by accident. (This one is particularly impressive, as I'm sure you would agree if you have a dog of your own.)

Adam accomplished this last rule by training Jack to stay in a sit position with food set out in front of him. Adam removed the food if Jack broke his sit without permission. When Jack stayed in his sit position and waited for Adam to release him, he was rewarded with the food. Adam said this wasn't hard for Jack to learn, and he learned it in a couple of days.

What made Jack's relationship with Adam and Carrie special was the trust they had developed between them. Adam said trust was at the core of their relationship, and Jack has had to earn it. Jack, for his part, has done some pretty interesting things to demonstrate he's trustworthy.

One time Adam convinced Jack that it was safe for him to climb an eight-foot ladder. Jack didn't want to do it. But Adam convinced him that he wouldn't ask Jack to do something that would hurt him. (How he did this I'm not sure, but humans and dogs have their own special ways of communicating.) Jack climbed the ladder and Adam helped him get down.

Another time Jack got out of the yard when someone accidentally left the gate open. Jack walked two miles through the downtown area, crossing an expressway and several busy streets to Adam's office.

Apparently, Jack had been snacking along the way (we can only imagine). When he arrived, one of Adam's colleagues noticed that Jack looked like a sausage, he had eaten so much. That didn't last long. Jack promptly deposited his snacks in the middle of the floor.

Adam says Jack talks to them all the time, only they're not always sure what Jack is saying. Adam has learned to listen to Jack and try to figure out his messages.

With two principles in place – set the rules and follow the rules – their relationship has had the foundation of trust it has needed to flourish. Adam told me that he's followed those principles life and at work. Great relationships are based on trust and mutual learning, at home or on the job.

Developing a good relationship with your dog can take time. My business partner Jim Ramerman's relationship with his dog, Terra, a beautiful Golden Retriever, has had its ups and downs, to say the least.

Jim and His Faithful Companion (In His Own Words)

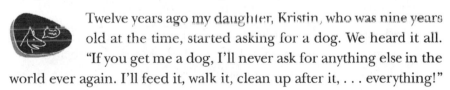

Twelve years ago my daughter, Kristin, who was nine years old at the time, started asking for a dog. We heard it all. "If you get me a dog, I'll never ask for anything else in the world ever again. I'll feed it, walk it, clean up after it, . . . everything!"

My wife, Mary, was supporting Kristin in her quest. I was ambivalent at best. Three kids and a demanding consulting practice had me all but overwhelmed. I believed I was in the "consideration stage."

Apparently, Mary and Kristin thought I was in the "committed" stage (which might go a long way in explaining lots of miscommunications between men and women, now that I think about it) because to my surprise, I came home one evening to find a Golden Retriever puppy sitting in my kitchen. I was stunned. How was I going to explain to them that this was unacceptable? I found out that the puppy came with papers; she was a purebred Golden Retriever. They paid more than $500 for her! An animal that I hadn't even committed to owning!

Money was very tight in those days. I believed if we were going to get a dog at all, it should be a mutt, like the one I had when I was a kid. Hogan had been half Basset, quarter Cocker, and quarter Spaniel – a real community project. Still, once the dog was in our house, sitting right there in our kitchen, how could I say no? It would have broken their hearts.

I suggested the name Terra, and though I'm not always given credit, the name stuck. So I suppose that was one connection I had with her – the first one. In general, Terra and I got off on the wrong foot. I had some resentment. I didn't want to do anything for the dog, as beautiful as she was.

A few months into her life, a crisis occurred. My daughter Kristin was holding a stick in her hand, way above her head, while playing with Terra in the backyard. Terra, tiny pup that she was, tried to leap the five feet to get it. Not even close. But she came down wrong on her leg, yelped, and squirmed in pain on the ground.

I had watched the whole thing. Although I'd never thought of myself as great in emergencies, I did my best. I took charge and took care of Terra. We got her to the vet and into her cast, the first of several. Pink. Green. Blue. One new cast at $100 a pop was needed each week because she was growing so fast. I was suddenly getting more emotionally (and financially) involved with Terra.

The family had a tough time getting Terra to obey. I think they loved her too much. I wasn't addicted. I had some emotional distance. I'm six-feet, two-inches tall, and I have a big voice when I need it. I could control her. I became the alpha male.

Somehow, over the years, Terra and I have grown closer and closer. She needed me and I responded to her. Golden Retrievers are number one among dogs in my book when it comes to affection, both for needing and giving it. She always loved me, no matter how hard I tried to distance myself.

She waits every day for me to come home and feed her. I pretend to still resent it, but of course, I don't. Now that she's twelve and in her "golden" dog years, I know I don't have much more time with her. She still looks beautiful. I treasure every moment we share together. She is Terra, my dog and my friend.

To quote Paul McCartney, "Sometimes love happens in an instant – sometimes it doesn't come at all." With Terra, love came in its own good time. I'm not sure anyone has ever written a song about that, have they? Anyway, I'm very glad that it happened.

Assertion is Key

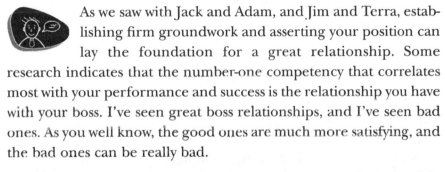 As we saw with Jack and Adam, and Jim and Terra, establishing firm groundwork and asserting your position can lay the foundation for a great relationship. Some research indicates that the number-one competency that correlates most with your performance and success is the relationship you have with your boss. I've seen great boss relationships, and I've seen bad ones. As you well know, the good ones are much more satisfying, and the bad ones can be really bad.

More things tend to go right when you have a good relationship with your boss, and the inevitable problems that occur aren't as difficult to resolve. When your boss trusts you and you know that your boss has "got your back," you can work with more confidence and less worry.

Very few things tend to go right when you have a bad relationship with your boss, and your situation can easily become a self-perpetuated failure. When you don't trust and respect each other, judgments form and resentments kick in.

The question, though, is how do you get a great relationship with your boss? Is it chemistry? Does it have to be based on friendship? Is it luck? I don't think it's the last two, or any one thing in particular, but chemistry certainly helps.

The relationship you have with your boss takes attention, understanding, and a dedication to make it work (like any good marriage). It takes time. It also takes a key skill on your part: assertion.

Assertion is the expression of your thoughts and feelings to another individual so you can achieve your needs. This should be done without infringing upon the rights and needs of another and without harming the other's self-esteem. You need to be direct, but sensitive. Assertion is <u>not</u> aggression, where you meet your needs at the expense of others. Developing your assertion skills will help you:

- Teach others how you want to be treated.

- Develop deeper interpersonal relationships.

- Build your self-esteem.

- Get your needs met (without harming others).

- Stand up for your human rights.

- Deal with your emotions.

- Solve problems and manage conflicts.

It's also important to work out and honor some basic rights with your boss. Try to negotiate these early. They may include:

- Being listened to with respect.

- Being assertive, expressing yourself, and meeting your personal goals.

- Refusing requests and saying "no" when appropriate without feeling guilty or selfish.

- Requesting what you want from the other person.

- Making mistakes and taking responsibility for them.

Execute a Strategy

 Ross had worked for Victor for less than two years. In that time their team had taken on a large project that Victor asked Ross to lead. The project grew in scope and magnitude, and Ross began to have more and more visibility with senior management and throughout the organization.

The project entailed a lot of meetings, as well as large levels of resource and budget allocation and forecasting, all of which played to Ross' strengths. He began making presentations to Victor and his peers for decision-making on a regular basis.

As the project progressed and the pressure to deliver climbed, the relationship between Victor and Ross became strained.

Victor supported Ross on his analysis. And Ross respected Victor's experience and leadership. But things didn't always go smoothly when it came time for Ross and his peers to deliver on their commitments. Some people didn't deliver on what they promised, and that made Victor frustrated and angry.

Ross would come to Victor in the beginning to let him know when he was running into problems. But he quickly found out that telling Victor about problems didn't always make them better, and sometimes made them worse. Victor would raise his voice when he heard about yet another problem.

"Ross, pick up the phone and call Rosalyn and tell her she has to come through on this! You just have to step it up and not let people run over you," Victor would say.

"Victor, I can't bully people into delivering on their commitments. That's not my style, and it never works anyway."

Ross would go to Victor's office, and his blood pressure would elevate before he ever even crossed the threshold. He started dreading the meetings. He knew Victor's way wasn't working. He knew that people were getting upset with Victor. He didn't want to let Victor down, and he was genuinely frustrated, too. He had to find a way to back Victor off and to get some latitude to solve the issues his way.

Ross and Victor had been my clients for a while, but I was working with Ross on this one. He wanted to have a better relationship with Victor, and I felt he had the motivation to do it. I also knew that Ross was a fast learner, so with the right focus, he could really make some positive changes in the relationship.

It helped that I knew them both, that I was familiar with their individual styles. I knew that Victor liked to be in control. He could be aggressive. He could also be directive. I also knew that Ross was strong analytically. He liked to be autonomous, and he was fairly introverted. It was important to both of them to be credible.

Ross grew cool and logical when Victor got hot and emotional. When Ross got mildly annoyed (he never really lost his temper), it was like lighting a keg of dynamite under Victor, and he got even hotter. When Victor tried to take control, Ross turned his frustration inward, felt devalued and angry that his boss didn't respect his abilities to resolve the situation.

Ross and I reviewed a couple of different strategies he might try with Victor, all of which would require new kinds of assertion from Ross. Ross was going to ask Victor what was important to him and what worried him when it came to solving problems. He would be better equipped to make the appropriate commitments to Victor if he understood these issues.

Then Ross was going to implement his best three-point plan:

1. Ask Victor not to direct solutions anymore.

2. Ask Victor to support Ross' own solutions.

3. Bring only 50 percent of the issues to Victor and solve the rest on his own.

Ross and I felt good about the plan and thought Victor would have a positive response to it. Ross began to see that the relationship could get better, and the tension began to drain away from his face. He could address the management and relationship issues directly, sensitively, and constructively, and achieve a positive outcome. Most important, he was willing to try.

High-Gain Insights

 People perform at higher levels when they have great relationships with their bosses. A person will stay in a job longer if a great relationship with a boss exists. Conversely, a person will leave earlier (or stay unhappily) when things don't mesh. As I said before, people don't leave companies, they leave people.

Sometimes the perception of differences in power can be an obstacle to developing great relationships with people at different levels inside and outside of your organization. Take our Power Gap^{SM} Assessment online at *www.LeadershipRising.com* to see how power affects your relationships.

Here are some Practical Ideas to help you build a good relationship with your boss:

- Take responsibility for the relationship with your boss.
- Understand your boss's expectations. Be specific and prioritize what's important.
- Find ways you can help your boss be successful.
- Shore up your boss's weaknesses.
- Be proactive. Make sure there are no surprises.
- Be challenging and encouraging at the same time.
- Communicate issues early – good news or bad.
- Give (and ask for) clarity in an unclear situation.
- Avoid "triangle-ing"[3] with or about your boss.

[3]One form of "triangling" is talking with someone about an issue you're having with someone else. When you involve a third person in a situation that can only be resolved with the original person, you risk complicating the situation, and potentially making the issue harder to resolve.

- Prepare to be autonomous. (forgiveness vs. permission)

- Be clear on your own goals and share them with your boss.

Ask or identify:

- To whom and for what is your boss responsible? List all the things for which your boss is responsible.

- How does your boss want information delivered?

- What does your boss see as success for you?

- Understand how your boss defines success.

- Know what is really important to both of you.

- What is your boss's work style? (collaborative vs. authoritarian)

- What pressures are you and your boss facing at work? (What keeps your boss awake at night?)

- What is your boss's communication style? Communicate with your boss in the style that person (or personality) needs.

There are a lot of powerful tips in these lists. Pick the one suggestion that you can do that will have the greatest positive impact on your relationship with your boss, and put it into action.

Diane Ravitch, an author and research professor of education at New York University, said, "The person who knows HOW will always have a job. The person who knows WHY will always be his boss."

Remember, by improving your relationship with your boss and by understanding your boss's problems, priorities, and goals, you will become a more valuable asset. If you want to advance and prosper at work, this is one of the best methods.

"If you are a dog and your owner suggests that you wear a sweater, . . . suggest that he wear a tail."

– FRAN LEBOWITZ

CHAPTER 18

A Secret About Leaders . . . They're Not Always Good at Developing People

Over the past ten years, we have worked with hundreds of CEOs and senior executives at private, public, and nonprofit organizations as they pursued higher levels of organizational performance and more effective leadership. We often gathered qualitative and quantitative feedback to help leaders gain insight into how their people experienced their leadership.

Thousands of participants providing feedback on hundreds of our executive clients have indicated that the skill of "developing people" is one of the top twenty most important skills for executive success. Yet, that skill is often rated lowest. A couple of years ago, The Conference Board reported that 40 percent of workers felt disconnected from their employers, and two out of every three workers couldn't identify with or feel motivated to drive their employer's business goals and objectives.

Clearly there's a disconnection between how important development is and how capable leaders are at providing it. That presents both a challenge and an opportunity. If you can't always rely on your company's leaders to provide you with effective development, you have to label it a priority and make it happen on your own.

One manager with whom I worked, David, received feedback from Human Resources and his team that he wasn't spending enough time teaching, coaching, and developing his people. The people who worked on his team were growing concerned about how their careers in the company might be affected. David wasn't generating as much loyalty within his team as he could have if he made more of an investment in their development.

The feedback was a wake-up call for him. I've rarely seen someone heed the call more fervently than David. He worked with me for more than a year on his own growth and development. He started giving a lot more feedback to his team, and he created a developmental atmosphere among his people and created new skill programs for them.

It was a joy to work with David and his team. Together we created a safe, open, learning environment. His team grew more comfortable with each other and began getting and giving constructive feedback. Humor and life were infused back into the team and their results showed it.

David recently received formal feedback from his Human Resources department and his team, and his ratings in development-focused leadership improved phenomenally. Through his focus and determination and the catalyst of the feedback he had received at the outset, he turned things around. What a great affirmation of the power of development!

You are likely to seek out new developmental opportunities for yourself if you're a highly learning-agile person. You'll go to seminars and classes, you'll read and learn. Maybe you already have a coach and a mentor. If you're a passive learner, which is true of 60 percent of the population according to a study by Lominger

International[4], you are less likely to make your development a priority and more likely to wait for someone else to suggest it. About 30 percent of the population is learning-blocked.

You may or may not believe strongly in the importance of your development or your capability for it. So here are some important principles to keep in mind when it comes to your development and growth at work:

1. <u>You're worth it and you deserve it!</u> No matter what position you have or aspire to, you need to put yourself at the top of the list.

2. <u>Don't fear change!</u> You may want to work for a long time, and there are many new changes you'll make and new things you'll learn along the way.

3. <u>You can do it!</u> Change can be scary if you let it be. The best way to build your confidence is to develop the knowledge and tools you'll need.

4. <u>You don't have to do it alone!</u> Seek support, input, and participation from others around you.

Many animal experts agree that dogs are capable of learning many things, but not all dogs are capable of learning all things. Dogs are motivated to please us, so they will keep trying when we present them with new learning opportunities. I've found this to be true with Scout, as well.

People are different from dogs when it comes to their learning and development. In order to be gainfully employed at something you love to do for a long time, which for most working people is an important part of survival, you will be required to continue learning, growing, and changing.

---

[4]Learning agility is your ability and willingness to learn new things. Lominger International indicates that 10 percent of the population is highly learning-agile; 60 percent of the population consists of passive learners, and 30 percent of the population is learning-blocked.

Blaze Becomes a Challenge

 I first met Blaze and his owner Karen when she was taking him for a walk on our street. I remember looking up and taking notice of a beautiful, distinctive-looking, and energetic puppy trotting toward me. I immediately walked into the street and introduced myself.

Blaze was a three-month-old, twenty-pound Australian Shepherd. He is merle colored, which means he has shades of red, tan, and white throughout his coat. What I first noticed when I met Blaze was his eyes; they are light green. With eyes more similar to those of a human rather than the typical dark eyes of dogs, Blaze looks alert and ready for action.

As I got to know Blaze, I realized how much he resembled his name.

Karen is a third-year medical resident in pediatric neurology at a hospital in our area. Her husband, Ken, is a physician's assistant at another hospital. As a physician-in-training, Karen is constantly in the position of learning and proving her knowledge to senior physicians. It's a toss up as to what's harder: becoming a good doctor or learning about herself when it comes to training Blaze. Both present challenges, some Karen expected and some she didn't.

Karen had dogs growing up. She lived with her grandparents for four years while her mother went to medical school. Karen recalls that her grandparents had a Siberian Husky who was a handful. He was undisciplined, untrained, and very smart. He would howl throughout dinner. One day he darted off when the door to the house was left open. He ran down the street and let his friend out by opening his gate so he'd have a companion to join in the fun.

When Karen rejoined her mother and stepfather, the family got a dog, a Terrier mix named Muffin. Muffin was a loving companion. But once again, the family made the mistake of not training the dog. Muffin was a leash-puller (I know that drill) and never came when called. One day when the family was out sailing and the water got a little rough, Muffin decided she'd had enough and jumped ship, thankfully landing on the dock three feet above the boat.

Karen knew she wanted a dog as an adult, but her husband Ken was more of a cat person. She had to convince Ken that a dog was a good idea. They looked at a lot of breeds: Retrievers, Poodles, and Labradors. Ken settled on an Australian Shepherd because he'd read that they were highly trainable and obedient. He liked this breed's personality. Karen was a bit concerned about the high energy levels of Australian Shepherds and the fact that they shed. But after finding a reputable breeder and meeting Blaze's parents, they chose Blaze, who seemed the calmest of the litter.

Blaze's calmness wore off after three days in his new home. He cried in his crate at night. Karen said it was hard for her to know what to do when he cried. She knew that she wasn't supposed to reward his crying by releasing him, but sometimes she was so tired or had to go to work and it was easier for her to end the howling by letting him out.

Karen was very enthusiastic about training Blaze, so she and Ken started in on obedience classes. At the first class, the instructor asked that the owners make sure their dogs didn't bark. Blaze, of course, barked throughout the class. He also jumped all around and relieved himself in the room.

"I felt that Blaze was the worst puppy in the class," Karen said. "Now I know how it must feel when your child misbehaves at school."

Blaze was on a leash next to us in the backyard while Karen and I sat and talked, and I got a small dose of what life with Blaze must be like. Here's a snapshot of what happened while I was there:

- Blaze chewed on the Adirondack chair upon which Karen was sitting.
- He ripped up wads of grass.

- He chewed relentlessly on a plastic pot.

- He ate and dug at the dirt in a planter.

- He couldn't bear it when he wasn't the center of attention, so he jumped up on both of us, depositing that dirt onto our clothes.

- He nipped at both of us constantly. His biting was exasperating for Karen, and she had a hard time talking because Blaze demanded so much of her attention.

At one point I put down my pad of paper and used the technique I learned from Cesar Milan. I grasped Blaze with my fingertips firmly but not painfully pressed into his muscles. For only a moment Blaze would calm down and then he would resume his antics.

Karen is finding out that she's being trained as much as she's training Blaze, and it's harder than she thought. She says that she's not as patient as she thought she was. She also never thought of herself as a leader, not as a physician, and not at home with Blaze.

Karen must exert her leadership with Blaze, because Blaze is testing her resolve and pushing the limits to see how far she'll let him go. Blaze is extremely smart and learns quickly, according to Karen. If you present him with a problem, Blaze tries to figure it out.

I have a feeling Karen is a lot like Blaze, she's extremely smart and learns quickly. With her conviction about the importance of training for herself and Blaze and her unwavering persistence, life will be a lot calmer six months from now once everyone in the household knows what to do and how to do it.

High-Gain Insights

Your development can take on many forms. It can be formal or informal. It can be in group settings or one-on-one. It can be cognitive or experiential A combination of targeted development is best. The important thing is to keep learning, growing, and developing. It will give you more options and a more stimulating career. Whenever possible, we like to use a combination of high-impact methods to maximize the development experience:

Here are some Practical Ideas that may help you enhance your potential at work:

- Feedback.

- Insight-generating instruments.

- Individual coaching.

- Group development programs inside and outside of the organization.

- New job or committee assignments.

- Mentoring.

Any one or a combination of these methods can be helpful to your development and can be made to fit into your time and financial budget.

The most important thing is that you get started doing something! Billionaire businessman Ted Turner said, "Lead, follow, or get out of the way." What position do you want to play?

"Anyone who stops learning is old, whether at twenty or eighty. Anyone who keeps learning stays young. The greatest thing in life is to keep your mind young."

– HENRY FORD

CHAPTER 19

Pace Yourself

I was feeling more confident that I had redefined my leadership role with Scout, and his indiscretions were becoming more manageable. So I asked Bob, our dog-trainer, for his advice on how to tackle the next issue: re-pacing my walks with Scout.

I loved walking Scout, or at least I thought I did. When we first got Scout, I did a lot more walking with him than I do today. My husband Terry walks him most of the time now. My son Matt and I walk him some of the time. It's the busyness of our work and school schedules that dictates the walking schedules.

So what's the big deal about walking a dog? Just put him on the leash and go, right? I used to think that way, too, until I realized that our walks weren't as pleasant as I thought they could be. Sometimes when I walked Scout, I was tired and my leadership signals were weak. We weren't walking in unison. Scout was outpacing me, and I spent a good deal of the time allowing Scout to tug me or tugging at the leash to redirect him.

I really loved the *idea* of walking Scout. You know, . . . me . . . the dog . . . the great outdoors . . . exercise . . . sunshine . . . joy!

Truth be told, Scout was a leash-puller. He got so excited about his walks that he was constantly tugging on the leash. Scout seemed to always know whose turn it was to walk him. He'd talk to us, gaze at us with his big, beautiful eyes, using a mind-meld technique he must have learned from Mr. Spock on *Star Trek*. He'd wag his white, fuzzy tail and follow the designated person around excitedly until it was time to go.

It was quite an undertaking for me just to get him ready for his walk. He'd hop around, pace, and toss his head back and forth while I would get his collar or harness around him. Then he'd step awkwardly into his stylish blue and green coat – an essential for a good part of the year in northern upstate New York – and then I'd apply his eye salve to keep those irritating road chemicals out of his eyes.

By the time we got outside, Scout's little motor was revving. He could barely contain himself as I carried him onto the part of the driveway past the crack that indicated we were outside of the hidden-fence zone. As soon as we reached the end of the driveway and I'd put him down, Scout would lurch for our mailbox, and his target shooting (peeing) would begin.

He then tugged me for the remainder of the walk, alternately pulling the lead toward anything that interested him: mailboxes, other dogs, people, bicycles, cars, plants, and trees. I had been his somewhat willing partner for years.

There were several things wrong with this picture.

First, Scout's constant yanking against his lead was putting pressure on his neck, compressing his nerves, and potentially contributing to glaucoma in his left eye.

He was likely coming home frustrated and exhausted and probably uncomfortable after pulling me along for the entire walk. I was the obstacle getting in the way of him having fun on his walk, the joy he looked forward to each day, and that couldn't be good.

I felt as if we were having twenty-minute tug-of-war contests instead of walks. Scout was winning, and I was losing my patience. Will Rogers once said, "Diplomacy is the art of saying 'Nice doggie' until you can find a rock." That was pretty much the way Scout was making me feel.

So the questions I asked myself were: OK, who is walking whom? Who's the boss? Why have I been allowing Scout to take me for a walk for so many years instead of me taking him? I was ready for the roles to reverse. I went to Bob, and we went to work.

Bob taught me some new techniques for walking Scout. He suggested I buy a six-foot lead and use a new collar for Scout that had flexible plastic points instead of the nylon collar I had been using. It would be gentler on Scout's neck and wouldn't put as much pressure on his eyes.

I'd trained Scout to follow my "sit," "stay," and "down" commands. He did a great job following those cues in the house, but once we got outside, he'd get distracted and not act as compliant on all of them.

I held the six-foot lead with some slack, as Bob suggested, keeping about a foot or so in a loop. I expected Scout to stay within four feet of me and to keep pace. I no longer tugged the lead. When he pulled out ahead of me or fell behind by more than four feet, I'd let the loop go and quickly pop or jerk the lead. As I jerked the lead, I'd turn around and walk in the opposite direction.

By the time Scout turned around he would see my back. He didn't associate the correction with me because we didn't make eye contact. Then he walked up beside me and looked into my eyes for approval, and I set the new pace.

At the beginning of trying out this new method, it was a pretty funny picture. We would walk a few feet, and I'd have to jerk the lead and reverse. Then we'd walk a few feet the other way, and I'd have to the jerk the lead and reverse again. We did a lot of walking back and forth, covering the same territory over and over again, before Scout got the message.

Now we can cover more ground, but I still have to make the reverse move every time he tests my resolve. He looks at me several times along the way to confirm that his pace is right, and I give him a big "good boy!" to let him know he's on the mark.

I also give Scout a "stay" command two or three times during our walks. He stops until I say "OK," and then he knows he can resume walking at my pace. I learned that by making some simple but clear changes with Scout, I could re-pace him and be more in charge. Scout responded so quickly that it surprised me.

Walks have been a lot more fun for both of us now that we understand our roles and requirements, and I've given him feedback along the way.

Who's In Charge of Your Time?

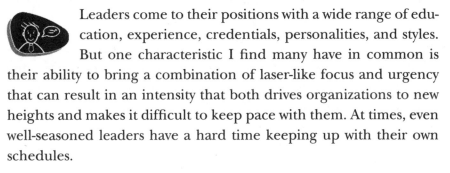 Leaders come to their positions with a wide range of education, experience, credentials, personalities, and styles. But one characteristic I find many have in common is their ability to bring a combination of laser-like focus and urgency that can result in an intensity that both drives organizations to new heights and makes it difficult to keep pace with them. At times, even well-seasoned leaders have a hard time keeping up with their own schedules.

Re-pacing yourself, whether we're talking about recalculating the rate of change a team or an entire organization can absorb, or merely how we manage the time we have in a day, is a critical skill to learn for the well-being of the leader and the people around that key person.

In Doug's case, re-pacing became a pivotal decision for the welfare of the organization and his own career. One day Doug arrived at my office for our regularly scheduled meeting and I immediately sensed we were going to have a deep conversation. I saw Doug about every six-to-eight weeks. Always well-dressed, he made a habit of arriving quietly, in a full suit and tie. An athletic man, Doug would rise at 4:00 a.m., run several miles, start work at his home computer by around 6:00 a.m., and arrive at his first meeting of the day or at his desk by 7:00 a.m.

He said he didn't need much sleep, but on this particular day he seemed tired. Evening appointments, dinner engagements, and socializing typically meant about sixteen-hour days for Doug. Long days are not unusual for top executives. The issue for Doug wasn't the number of hours he worked; the issue was what it was like to be in a meeting with him. From what I could determine from our talks, Doug's style was wearing everyone out, even Doug.

Doug was well-respected in his organization and in the community. He was always in demand. He made his mark as an agent for change, and always asked challenging questions. He thought big. He had vision and was influential.

After his 4:00 a.m. run and early start, here's what a typical day looked like for Doug:

7:00–12:00	Four or five back-to-back meetings or an all-morning meeting
12:00–1:00	Working lunch appointment
1:00–5:30	Four or five back-to-back meetings or an all-afternoon meeting
6:00–8:00	Working dinner appointment
8:30–10:00	Home
10:00–11:00	Catch-up on reading and e-mails

Doug was famous for his drill-downs. If you were in a business review with Doug, you didn't want to be caught short on your facts and details about a situation. He loved to "grill and fry his catch," all in the name of toughening you up. His intentions were good but his methods were questionable.

With almost no time between meetings, Doug was left with precious little thinking time, which did not play to his needs. While most people assumed Doug loved to be around people, and he spent almost all of his time doing just that, Doug was in fact an introvert and actually required much more thinking and alone time than he ever got. Because he lacked time on his own to recharge, Doug was often a bit edgy in meetings.

In one meeting, he chastised his assistant in front of other executives for making a spelling error. In another meeting with an outside consultant, he spoke so fast trying to cram all the information he could into fifteen minutes, he overwhelmed the person, who never had a chance to ask a question. The stakes got higher; his boss was beginning to get reports that Doug was out of touch with his organization.

Doug was so focused on the endgame, he wasn't seeing how the organization was struggling. He was trying to make so many changes in the organization at once; projects were starting to get off-track; people were being over-taxed and stressed-out; and he wasn't listening when people were trying to tell him there were problems.

I told Doug he looked pretty tired and let that settle in for a moment. Then I asked him, "How do you think your intensity is playing out in the organization?"

"We all know I'm impatient with the rate of change," Doug replied, chuckling a bit. He stirred in his seat, shifted his weight, and leaned back in the black high-back chair in my office.

"You keep quite a hectic schedule. I'm wondering if you're getting enough time to think things through before going into meetings. I don't think you're listening well. I can't imagine people are enjoying your meetings lately."

"Definitely not," he said. "I don't control half the meetings on my schedule. They just appear. My secretary tries to give me a little breathing room but the organizational demands are just too high."

"So who's in charge of your time?" I asked with a joking lilt in my voice.

"OK, OK, I get it. I'd better start changing my calendar. To be honest, I'm starting to feel as tired as I look. I guess it's time to do something about it."

I wondered if Doug was sincere or just trying to get me out of his hair, which, by the way, was fairly common among my high-powered clients.

But Doug has held to his promise for the last few months. He sat down with his secretary and built in more thinking time and, whenever possible, has scheduled fewer meetings in a day. He's starting to address the problems to which people have been so desperately trying to draw his attention. He's beginning to realize that his personal habits are important to his professional life. They're big issues but he isn't daunted. He may, in fact, have to rethink the timetable for some of his projects, but he's ready and willing to do the hard work.

Doug's days are still long, but re-pacing himself has decreased his intensity levels. He even takes a few minutes to talk casually with people at the beginning of his meetings. He seems happier and less stressed. I'm sure his people are, too. (Now if we could only get those sixteen-hour days cut down a bit. But, that'll have to wait for another time.)

High-Gain Insights

 If you want to pace yourself better at work, there are three elements that might help you hit your stride:

1. **Realization:** Organizations want a lot of your time if you'll give it. It's not that the organizations are bad, it's just that there's a lot to do, fewer people to get it done, and urgent deadlines to meet.

2. **Leadership:** You can assertively and positively take more charge of your time by connecting with key people around you and letting them know you're committed for the long term.

3. **Consistency:** Organizations aren't always sure what to make of change, so you'll need to positively reinforce it to make it stick.

Here are some Practical Ideas for re-pacing at work. You can start by honestly asking yourself these questions:

- How much time are you really spending working (inside and outside of work)?

- How much of that time is truly productive?

- How much time are you giving to people and things outside of work that are important to you?

- Are you experiencing any health problems from the pace of your work?

Create a plan of what you would have to do at work to be more in charge of your time.

- Specifically determine a pace that would provide real value to your employer as well as be at a manageable level for you.

- Assess the risks of not re-pacing yourself.

- Determine who you would have to talk to.

- Asses the risks and benefits of negotiating a re-pacing for yourself.

- Practice what you will say and how you will say it. Remember, there are a lot of skills that you can apply from Chapter 9, "If You Want to Have Fewer Conflicts, Have More of Them" and Chapter 10, "Enhancing Your Clarity."

- Have the conversation(s) you need to have.

Discovering your pace at work and making changes when you need to may be one of the greatest gifts you can give yourself.

Buddha said, "Health is the greatest gift, contentment, the greatest wealth." The following are a couple of important considerations:

- If you are not in charge of your pace and you can't negotiate a re-pacing, you'll have to find ways to stay healthy by being creative and disciplined in your current environment. If that's not possible, then Chapter 20, "Is It Time to Move On?" may apply.

- If you are the one creating an unproductive or unhealthy pace for yourself, then that's the person with whom to "have a conversation." You may need support from your supervisor, coach, or other professional. If you are making yourself unhealthy, you serve yourself and others by working with an EAP (Employee Assistance Program) or a similar resource.

"If a dog will not come to you after he has looked you in the face, you should go home and examine your conscience."

–WOODROW WILSON

CHAPTER 20

Is It Time
to Move On?

Jamie is a special client and fellow dog enthusiast. He came to my office one day to tell me the story of having to make the decision to put his beloved dog Roxie down, and what he learned about himself during this heart-wrenching process.

He told me this story while he was still very emotional about it, shortly after Roxie's death.

Jamie Learns a Lesson in Life (In His Own Words)

 Roxie was a cross between a German Shepherd and a Redbone Coonhound. She was a ten-year-old, seventy-pound hunting dog with tremendous prey drive.

We got her to keep our other dog, Opus, company. Roxie was timid and shy when she first joined our family. She had a problem with fear and aggression. Opus was the dominant one. She got along best with Opus and did well with the rest of us, but she had a problem with other dogs and people outside the family.

After Opus died, Roxie's fear and aggression seemed to subside, and she started to relax a bit. She became more affectionate with people and dogs, and seemed to discover some measure of playfulness and peace within herself.

One night in the summer of 2005, Roxie developed a severe pain. Her stomach was bloated. On the X-ray, the vet found that Roxie's stomach had "twisted," and that she had a large chest mass. Roxie would need two surgeries, the first to correct the twisted stomach – the bloat – and the second to remove the mass.

There was never any doubt in my mind that I would ask the vet to do whatever she could to save Roxie. I had grown to love Roxie, as had our entire family, so I scheduled the surgeries and nervously awaited the outcomes.

Roxie recovered from her first procedure, the stomach surgery, fairly well. During the second procedure, the surgeon removed two pounds of tumor from her chest. It was a relief to know that Roxie had survived such a difficult surgery at all, but the good news was not to last. Her prognosis wasn't good. The vet informed me that Roxie had a form of bone cancer. For a short time, five months – which I viewed as a gift every single day – Roxie rallied, but then she began coughing. Within a few days, she noticeably thinned out. The tumor had grown back and was much larger than before.

On a cold, bright day in the middle of January, I gathered the family together to tell them it was time to put Roxie to sleep. I'm not unaccustomed to making hard decisions. I'm a physician and head of a medical practice. As part of my work, I know what it's like to have to give patients difficult diagnoses and to make hard decisions, professionally, that profoundly affect the lives of others. But this decision was going to touch everyone in our immediate family on a very intimate level.

I made a point to spend time with Roxie on her last day. Once my wife and I arrived at the vet's office, I was pretty clear about and at peace with our decision, although the whole thing was still kind of surreal. I don't remember much of what happened at the vet's office. I just remember leaving there without Roxie.

My wife and I helped our children with their sorrow. When a dog dies a natural death, like Opus did, it's different. You grieve, but you don't have to deal with the weight of the decision, of knowing it was you who put an end to the life of a beloved companion.

If I was pressed into saying that something good had come out of the experience, I guess I'd say that I learned some things about myself through this lifecycle event that I could apply in my life and in my work. First of all, I learned that making hard calls can be stressful and overwhelming at times, but it's worse not to make those calls at all. Also, in making this hard decision with Roxie and seeing the impact it had on my family, I noticed that my wife gained insight into some of the difficulties I face in my work life, and I gained additional clarity regarding my role as CEO and physician.

Things don't work out all the time, and as a physician, business leader, husband, and father, I understand the hardships and consequences that go along with that. Finally, I feel blessed to have become a physician and to be in a position to make a meaningful difference in the lives of my patients.

A few weeks later I saw Jamie at a classical music concert. He proudly pulled out pictures of the latest family addition, Sydney, a rescued German Shepherd puppy. When I finally got a chance to speak to Jamie about it later, he said, "I was missing the loving spirit a dog brings to me. A dog is someone to share life's experiences with, the good times and the bad times. The incredible bond I have with dogs makes me whole. Having a dog completes me."

What Clients Say About Moving on at Work

Leaving a company is not exactly a life-and-death experience, as Jamie went through with Roxie, but it can feel like one, depending on how it happens. In my opinion, it's right up there with moving, divorce, and death on the list of the most stressful occurrences in life. And moving on doesn't necessarily mean leaving your company. It could mean changing jobs within a company.

For my clients who have left their companies or are considering it, the issue isn't usually leaving too soon – it's staying in a job too long.

The decision to leave can be stressful. There's doubt, uncertainty, change, fear, and second-guessing. It's all there. But we have a choice, and that choice is to either let our doubts and insecurities stop us, or to take a risk when we know in our hearts it's the right thing to do.

The great actor Harrison Ford once said about his decision to pursue acting, "Acting was a way out at first. A way out of not knowing what to do, a way of focusing ambitions. And the ambition wasn't for fame. The ambition was to do an interesting job." If he hadn't taken that step, I wonder what he would have become.

It's important to look at a major decision from many different angles, but some people, overwhelmed by the decision, forget to consult their instincts. It's easy to squash your subconscious by rationalizing endlessly (or just plain thinking it to death). Sigmund Freud once said, "When making a decision of minor importance, I have always found it advantageous to consider all the pros and cons. In vital matters, however, such as the choice of a mate or a profession, the decision should come from the unconscious, from somewhere within ourselves."

Here are some crutches people I know have used to avoid change. See if any of them sound familiar:

"Maybe I should stick it out."

"It could be a lot worse."

"I'll give it another six months."

"I've got responsibilities. How could I be thinking of making a move now?"

"Does this make sense to do at my age?"

"I haven't been in the job market in ten years."

"What if I can't make as much money?"

"What if we have to move?"

"What kind of job could I get?"

"Maybe my boss will leave and things will get better."

"I don't like change."

"I'm afraid."

What I'm <u>not</u> hearing is that it's time for them to move on because:

"I don't like what I'm doing anymore."

"I'm bored to tears."

"I love what I'm doing, but my boss and I don't get along."

"I love what I'm doing, but I don't like the culture."

"I like the work; it's the people who are the problem."

"I hate coming in here every day."

"I'm burned out."

"I'm not growing anymore."

"I'm not making an impact."

The Right Thing at the Right Time

 Sam, one of my longtime clients, had been managing the same department for more than fifteen years. Sam was a dedicated company man. He was well-respected and liked, and had a reputation for being a thoughtful decision-maker and a good listener. He knew the people in the company and in his department very well, and many of them were his friends.

While the department had grown quite a bit, in some respects, Sam hadn't changed a lot within his job. He struggled to make the department profitable. Morale wasn't as good as it once was, and the work wasn't being managed well enough. There were write-offs and cost overruns, and it was harder to get a handle on all the issues and correct them.

Over a period of several years, Sam and I worked together to make improvements. Slowly some progress occurred, but there was never a big breakthrough. Sam was a patient man, so he never got discouraged with the rate of progress.

From time to time I would ask Sam whether he thought he was the right man for the job at this stage in the department's evolution. Sam would just nod his head and say he thought so. Change wasn't something he would consider or vocalize, and we'd move on in the conversation.

Sam's boss, Rick, had a lot of respect for Sam and genuinely liked him. Sam was like a counselor to Rick on a lot of company matters. Rick always supported Sam even when Sam's department performed at subpar levels.

But one day Rick suggested to Sam that he'd like him to take on a special-projects role as an individual contributor and let someone else do the heavy lifting in the department. Sam understood what Rick was saying and supported Rick's decision.

Sam has gone on to his new job and is doing it with vigor. Someone else is now running the department, and although Rick is finding out that problems are not so easily fixed, both men feel as if the change was the right thing at the right time for everyone.

Ah, Clarity

 Marilyn and her boss Tamara weren't getting along, and everyone on the team knew it. Marilyn was an energetic go-getter. She sometimes stepped on toes in her pursuit of results. She'd always been a solid performer, but she'd made a couple of missteps.

One time she overstepped her authority and requested some work be done outside the company without Tamara's approval. Tamara got upset. Another time she spoke out at a meeting and disagreed with Tamara. Tamara was not happy about it.

Rather than give Marilyn feedback about the issues, Tamara let them simmer. She didn't like conflict. She thought Marilyn would get the message. Marilyn didn't.

Instead, Tamara changed the way she treated Marilyn. She started giving assignments to other team members that typically would have gone to Marilyn. She stopped having one-on-one meetings with Marilyn. Marilyn grew confused and nervous. She didn't understand Tamara's abrupt change and was afraid to confront her about it.

Communications between Tamara and Marilyn had nearly broken down by the time we started working together. When I asked the team what they thought about the situation, they said they were upset with both of them for letting this go on for so long. They didn't like the position in which they were putting the rest of the team. They felt Marilyn was wrong for overstepping her authority, and they also felt Tamara was wrong for freezing Marilyn out. Team meetings became tense, and nobody wanted to come anymore.

I asked Tamara what she wanted to do.

"I'm ticked off at Marilyn. I want her to apologize and not to do those things again," she replied.

"Do you want to keep her in her position?" I asked.

"Yes," she said, "but she'll have to change."

I asked Marilyn what she wanted to do.

"I can't believe Tamara couldn't tell me these things earlier. I've been in the dark for six months. Does she want me to stay or go?"

"Do you want to stay and work on things?" I asked.

"I don't know. I have to think about it," Marilyn replied.

So time went on. Tamara gave Marilyn an occasional project. They had a short meeting once in a while. The situation eased up a bit, but things never really changed, and neither of them healed or forgave the other.

Marilyn would come to my office and always dutifully go through the paces. We worked on the lessons she needed to learn from the missteps she'd made. But it never seemed as if her heart was in it.

Tamara and I continued to meet periodically. She was often late for appointments, usually in a hurry, running from one meeting to the next. We continued to work on the way she managed her people.

When I would ask how Marilyn was doing, she would say, "OK," followed by a remark like, "I'm not sure she'll ever quite get it." I felt like we made small strides but never large leaps.

Tamara didn't ask Marilyn to go. Marilyn didn't ask Tamara whether she should stay.

Then one day, Marilyn came to my office for our appointment. She looked more relaxed and at peace with herself than I'd seen her in a long time. She was smiling.

"I've made an important decision," she said. "I'm leaving the company. I've decided it's time to move on. I've wanted to make a change for some time now, try out some other things I'm interested in. How do you think I should tell Tamara?"

Ah, clarity.

"Tell her early. Help her make the transition to a new person smoothly. Offer to help her in any way you can. Do it with your head held high and with integrity," I said.

And that's exactly what Marilyn did. She's gone on to a new job with another company. Reports are that she's much happier.

Tamara is still working on her management skills.

High-Gain Insights

 If you're thinking about whether you're in the right position or the right company, it's important that you become clear on the issues so you can address them realistically, in the right way, and make the best decisions. John Chambers, President and CEO of Cisco Systems, Inc., said, "Deal with the world the way it is, not the way you wish it was." This is sound advice for anyone thinking about making a job or career change.

Commitment, loyalty, conflict resolution, and perseverance are all admirable qualities or skills. They are essential for long-term ethical success. Still, a time comes when the healthiest choice to make, for both the individual and the organization, is to move on. Consider the following signs to move on:

Signs	I experience this sign more often than not		Reflections
1. I get tenser the closer I get to my workplace.	Yes	No	
2. I am increasingly distracted at work.	Yes	No	
3. It's taking me longer and longer to do things.	Yes	No	
4. Nothing new excites me at work.	Yes	No	
5. I tried several different ways, but I can't change people's negative or limiting view of me.	Yes	No	
6. I can't find much or anything positive to say about my workplace.	Yes	No	
7. I consistently dream of being somewhere else and doing something different.	Yes	No	
8. I know what I want to do and resent my current employers and/or my employment situation.	Yes	No	

If you answered "yes" to the majority of questions one through five, it may be time to move on.

If you answered "yes" to question six, seven, or eight – any one of them – and the answer would be the same over a period of months (and you are not clinically depressed – a state that could make you feel this way about any position), it is no doubt time to move on.

When you become clear about moving on, that is a huge achievement. After all, change is difficult for most people, the disconnection from even a difficult situation is still a transition, and the anxiety about finding a new position can be great, often overwhelming. Now the goal is to make the change. Here are some tips:

- Determine your own goals, your talents, your motivation, the kind of work you want to do, the kind of boss you want to work for.

- Think about what you have learned from your current work experience, what you want to hang onto, and what you want to let go.

- Put a plan together: how to exit your current position gracefully; how to network and search for a new position that fits.

- Have the courage to make the change. And then move on.

"If you don't place your foot on the rope, you'll never cross the chasm."
— ANONYMOUS

"We accept the verdict of the past until the need for change cries out loudly enough to force upon us a choice between the comforts of further inertia and the irksomeness of action."
— LOUIS L'AMOUR

CHAPTER 21

Why Dogs Wag Their Tails

"The reason a dog has so many friends is that it wags its tail instead of its tongue."

—ANONYMOUS

Watching a happy dog wag its tail does wonders for the human soul. A happy dog radiates joy. You can see it in the way it shivers with excitement. You can see it in the way its entire body pitches from side to side from the sheer force of its thrashing tail. You can see the sparkle in its eyes. And this euphoric mutt, this amazingly compact manufacturer of absolute delight, does all of this for you, because *your* dog is happy to see you, *your* dog loves you in a way that only dogs can love.

Is it any wonder that we love our dogs so much?

A dog's tail – a length of seven tightly corded muscles gripping a string of tiny bones – is a remarkable thing. A dog can control it like a precision instrument. Nowadays, most dog experts agree that dogs use tail-wagging to send social signals, to communicate a wide range of emotions to humans and other dogs.

Psychologist and dog trainer Dr. Stanley Coren, from *How to Speak Dog*, says, "A dog will wag its tail for a person or another dog.

It may wag its tail for a cat, horse, mouse, or perhaps even a butterfly. But when the dog is by itself, it will not wag its tail to any lifeless thing. This is one indication that tail-wagging is meant as communication or language. In the same way that we don't talk to walls, dogs don't wag their tails to things that are not apparently alive and socially responsive."

Dogs may also be trying to tell us very important things when they wag their tails, like their rank within a social order. According to Dwight Tapp, a PhD candidate in psychology at the University of Toronto, "A dominant dog will often display an aggressive wag – a tail held high and wagging slightly – when confronted by a dog or person it does not know. Low-ranking dogs, on the other hand, will often begin a new exchange with their tails between their legs, wagging only slightly."

In fact, the more we study dogs, the more we learn from them. The wag of a tail carries plenty of subtleties in meaning. A brief, swift tail wag may indicate a moment of recognition, as if the dog was saying, "Hey, I remember you." A slow wag of the tail may reflect a dog's uncertainty or confusion. When a dog holds its tail up and curved, it's an expression of dominance. The tail held down, near the hind legs, is a gesture of insecurity. Short, fast strokes may mean aggression or fear.

It's clear that dogs have much to tell us. I've learned a lot from Scout, from watching him and trying to read his social signals, and from talking to him and trying to get him to understand mine. One of the reasons I wrote this book was because I have come to realize that if we humans can learn the simplest of things from our dogs – how to live in the moment, how to find joy in everyday life, and how to exist without artifice – we can all be much happier at home and at work, and so can those around us.

Humans and dogs have lived together for 14,000 years. The innate ability our canine companions possess to communicate with us is one of the major reasons why we've gotten along so wonderfully for so long. Dogs view us as an extension of their own tribe. They've learned how to interpret our moods, minds, and complicated needs. Dogs, without even realizing it, have helped us live better lives.

So along with all of the sound business advice my business partner – Jim Ramerman – and I have laid out for you in this book, along with the High-Gain Insights we've asked you to consider, the questions we've encouraged you to answer, and the stories we've invited you to read, I hope you will also come to see how much our dogs have to teach us about finding joy in our lives and work.

I hope you'll actually take some of the steps we've recommended, implement them, and pass along your new approaches to friends, family, and colleagues as you see good results happening, and help them to apply these principles in their own lives.

By your clear and thoughtful actions, you can become more effective and happier. You can help to create healthy and productive cultures in which you and other people will want to work. You can find or rekindle your passion for your job and career.

In the end, if you haven't done so already, you may even begin to see dogs for the amazing creatures they are. I know I have. And it has helped me immeasurably.

Let's celebrate with our dogs when they wag their tails. You have nothing to lose . . . and everything to gain.

"You can buy a pretty good dog with a lot of money, but you can't buy the wag of its tail."

–JOSH BILLINGS

Catalysts, Insights, and Santa Barbara

The journey that led to this book began on a walk along the beach in Santa Barbara, California, with Elaine, a friend of my brother. Elaine is a successful and now happily retired author. I described to her my passion for work, for dogs, and my ideas for this book. As we walked and talked, she became increasingly excited about the concept, too. It was an unexpected High-Gain conversation, and it really got my juices flowing.

Her enthusiastic encouragement was infectious. By the end of our time together, it was clear that I could and *would* write this book. When I returned home, I focused and started planning how I would get it done.

There were the inevitable obstacles to overcome. I had a lot of research to do. I didn't have much time in my hectic schedule to do it. And I would have to make choices about the direction for the book and prepare an outline.

I did the research and hired a wonderful editor, Nick DiChario. Nick kept up with me and gave me encouraging and direct feedback all along the way. He also gave me a pep talk when I needed it.

Without him, this book would never have been developed to the level he helped me take it.

At Elaine's suggestion, I set aside several weeks to go off on a writing retreat. It's no wonder that when I was choosing a place to write the book, I decided to come back to Santa Barbara, where the idea had first picked up steam. It's a beautiful town with a temperate climate right on the ocean, and there are lots of dogs!

I found a lovely bungalow, owned by Faye and Victor, where I stayed to write the majority of the manuscript. What a delightful couple and great hosts they turned out to be. We became friends during the time I was there. They invited me for brunch at their home and took good care of me during my stay. The bungalow was very comfortable. It was located less than a mile from State Street, the main shopping area. It reminded me of my brother's house when he had lived in Santa Barbara years ago.

The bungalow had two bedrooms, a small kitchen, and a living-room/dining-room area. I positioned my work table at the front window overlooking the porch, the front garden, and of course the street, where I could watch the people of Santa Barbara go by, some walking with their children and their dogs. I could tell whether the person was walking the dog or the dog was walking the person, by the way. I'd had plenty of experience with both.

The time I was away on retreat went both quickly and slowly, a paradox I'm wrestling with to this day. I slowly, arduously worked my way through each word and each chapter. Yet, when I look back on it now, the time seemed to pass so quickly, in a virtual blur. I stayed focused for the most part. But I had to bring a discipline to my days to make the progress I wanted. Writing is a learned skill for me, not a natural talent, and it requires a positive attitude and a daily schedule to keep me honest.

Nick and I stayed in touch just about every day. He edited quickly and turned chapters around at such a fast pace that I had no choice but to stay motivated and keep fully engaged in the writing process. It helped me so much to have his frequent feedback so I could make course corrections and apply what I learned to subsequent chapters.

Sometimes it took awhile to regain my focus if I let it slip. Sometimes, after focusing for a long period of time, my brain would get tired from concentrating. Thank heavens for my computer and the Internet. Nick tells me he still writes his drafts in longhand. I don't know how he does that.

The irony of having to go away to have uninterrupted, focused time to think and to write isn't lost on me when it comes to the reality of the workplace. It has actually been a good lesson for me. I now know that when it comes to completing a big project, I need more alone time than I usually get. I would go to bed thinking about a chapter I'd be in the midst of, and then I'd wake up with a fresh way to work on it. A delight!

It was also a great experience to be on my own. My family did beautifully without me, under the wonderful leadership of my husband, Terry. My son Matt said he missed my cooking. I missed them and I missed Scout. And I learned a number of things about myself:

I like to be by myself when I'm working on a project. I like to be around people, selectively, when I want to shop, sightsee, or have a meal; it's more fun to do those things with family and friends. I like a routine. I can live pretty simply. "Thinking time" is so important, and I don't get enough of it. Writing takes discipline, and there aren't any shortcuts. The best things in life aren't free, but earned. I have more than one book in me. And finally, if you get half as much out of my first book as I put into it, I will be a very, very happy author.

Please let me know if you're using the lessons in this book, how they're working for you, and what you're learning by contacting me through our Web site at *www.LeadershipRising.com.*

– SHERRI MCARDLE

Working with Sherri and Jim

Sherri McArdle and Jim Ramerman are available to provide results-focused CEO and executive development. They offer a variety of programs, including customized organizational consulting.

These nationally-recognized experts on leadership are exciting, informative and entertaining speakers.

For more information, please visit their web site, www.Leadership Rising.com.

REFERENCES

Beer, Michael and Eisenstat, Russell A. 2006. *How To Have an Honest Conversation About Your Business Strategy*. Harvard Business Review.

Bennis, Warren G. and Thomas, Robert J. 2002. *Geeks & Geezers: How era, values and defining moments shape leaders.* Harvard Business School Press

Bethanis, Susan J., EdD. 2004. *Leadership Chronicles of a Corporate Sage: Five keys to becoming a more effective leader.* Dearborn Publishing.

Blanchard, Kenneth. 1999. *The Heart of a Leader.* Honor Books.

Blanchard, Kenneth. 1998. *Gung Ho! Turning On the People in Any Organization.* William Morrow & Co.

Blanchard, Kenneth and Waghorn, Terry. 1997. *Mission Possible: Becoming a world-class organization while there's still time.* McGraw Hill.

Bolles, Richard N. 2000. *How to Find Your Mission in Life.* Ten Speed Press.

Bolles, Richard Nelson. 1998. *What Color is Your Parachute Workbook*. Ten Speed Press.

Bonham, Margaret H. 2005. *A Dog's Wisdom: A heartwarming view of life*. Howell Book House.

Bossidy, Larry and Charan, Ram. 2002. *Execution: The discipline of getting things done*. Crown.

Buckingham, Marcus and Clifton, Donald O. 2001. *Now, Discover Your Strengths*. Free Press.

Buckingham, Marcus and Coffman, Curt. 1999. *First, Break All the Rules: What the world's greatest managers do differently*. Simon & Schuster Inc.

Clifton, Donald and Nelson, Paul. 1992. *Soar with Your Strengths*. Dell Publishing.

Collins, Jim. 2001. *Good to Great*. Harper Collins Publishers.

Comella, Patricia. 1996. *Emotional Side of Organizations*. Georgetown Family Center.

Connors, Roger; Smith, Tom and Hickman, Craig. 2004. *The Oz Principal: Getting results through individual and organizational accountability*. Prentice Hall.

Covey, Stephen R. 1991. *Principle-Centered Leadership*. Simon & Schuster Inc.

Covey, Stephen R. 1989. *7 Habits Of Highly Effective People*. Simon & Schuster Inc.

DeGeus, Arie. 1997. *Living Company*. Harvard Business School Press.

Douglas, Katherine. 2003. *Dogma: Life lessons for dog lovers*. Barbour Publishing

Fisher, Roger and Ury, William L. 1991. *Getting to Yes: Negotiating agreement without giving in*. Penguin.

Fombrun, Charles J. 1996. *Reputation:* *Realizing value from the corporate image.* Harvard Business School Press.

Friedman, Edwin H. 1990. *Friedman's Fables.* Guilford Press.

Friedman, Edwin H. 1999. *A Failure of Nerve.* Edwin Friedman Estate.

Friedman, Thomas L. 2006. *The World Is Flat [Updated and Expanded]:* *A brief history of the twenty-first century.* Farrar, Straus and Giroux.

Gilbert, Roberta M. 1992. *Extraordinary Relationships: A New Way of Thinking About Human Interactions.* Chronimed Publishing.

Gladwell, Malcolm. 2005. *Blink:* *The power of thinking without thinking.* Little Brown and Company.

Goffee, Rob & Jones, Gareth. 2006. *Why Should Anyone Be Led by You?* *What it takes to be an authentic leader.* Harvard Business School Press.

Goleman, Daniel. 1995. *Emotional Intelligence.* Bantam Doubleday Dell Publishing Group.

Goleman, Daniel. 2000. *Working with Emotional Intelligence.* Bantam Doubleday Dell Publishing Group.

Hanh, Thich Nhat. 1991. *Peace is Every Step.* Bantam Doubleday Dell Publishing Group.

Hocker, Joyce L. and Wilmot, William W. 1985. *Interpersonal Conflict.* William C. Brown Publishers.

Kaplan, Robert S. and Norton, David P. 2001. *Strategy-Focused Organization.* Harvard Business School Press.

Katz, Neil H. and Lawyer, John W. 1985. *Communication and Conflict Management Skills.* Kendall/Hunt Publishing Company.

Kouzes, James M. and Posner, Barry Z. 1991. *Encouraging the Heart*. Jossey Bass Publishers.

Lencioni, Patrick M. 2002. *Five Dysfunctions of a Team: A leadership fable*. Jossey Bass Publishers.

Nomura, Catherine, Waller, Julia. 2003. *Unique Ability Creating the Life You Want*. Strategic Coach Inc.

O'Neill, Marybeth. 2000. *Executive Coaching with Backbone and Heart*. Jossey Bass Publishers.

Quinn, Robert E. 1996. *Deep Change: Discovering the leader within*. Jossey Bass Publishers.

Ritchey, Tom. 2002. *I'm Stuck, You're Stuck: Break through to better work relationships and results by discovering your disc behavioral style*. Berrett-Koehler Publishers.

Scott, Susan. 2002. *Fierce Conversations: Achieving success at work and in life, one conversation at a time*. Berkley Publishing.

The Monks of New Skete. 2003. *I & Dog*. Yorkville Press.

Tieger, Paul D. and Barron-Tieger, Barbara. 1992. *Do What You Are*. Little Brown and Company.

Index

WIN WEALTH WORTH WITH WBUSINESS BOOKS

Sales

First 100 Days of Selling: A Practical Day-by-Day Guide to Excel in the Sales Profession
ISBN 13: 978-0-8329-5004-9

By Jim Ryerson

Price: $22.95 USD

Soar Despite Your Dodo Sales Manager
ISBN 13: 978-0-8329-5009-4

By Lee B. Salz
Price: $19.95 USD

Great Salespeople Aren't Born, They're Hired: The Secrets to Hiring Top Sales Professionals
ISBN 13: 978-0-8329-5000-1

By Joe Miller

Price: $19.95 USD

Hire, Fire, & the Walking Dead: A Leaders Guide to Recruiting the Best
ISBN 13: 978-0-8329-5001-8

By Greg Moran with Patrick Longo
Price: $19.95 USD

Marketing

What's Your BQ? Learn How 35 Companies Add Customers, Subtract Competitors, and Multiply Profits with Brand Quotient
ISBN 13: 978-0-8329-5002-5

By Sandra Sellani

Price: $24.95 USD

Reality Sells: How to Bring Customers Back Again and Again by Marketing Your Genuine Story
ISBN: 978-0-8329-5008-7

By Andrew Corbus and Bill Guertin

Price: $19.95 USD

Entrepreneurship

The N Factor: How Efficient Networking and *Can Change the Dynamics of Your Business*
ISBN 13: 978-0-8329-5006-3

By Adrie Reinders Marion Freijsen

Price: $19.95 USD

Thriving Latina Entrepreneurs in America
ISBN 13: 978-0-8329-5007-0

By Maria de Lourdes Sobrino
Price: $24.95 USD

**Check out these books at your local bookstore or at
www.WBusinessBooks.com**

THIS BOOK DOESN'T END
AT THE LAST PAGE!

We want to hear from you!

Log on to **www.WBusinessBooks.com** and join the WBusiness community.

Share your thoughts, talk to the author, and learn from other community members in the forums. **www.WBusinessBooks.com** is a place where you can sharpen your skills, learn the new trends and network with other professionals.